# Make It Real

MW01247670

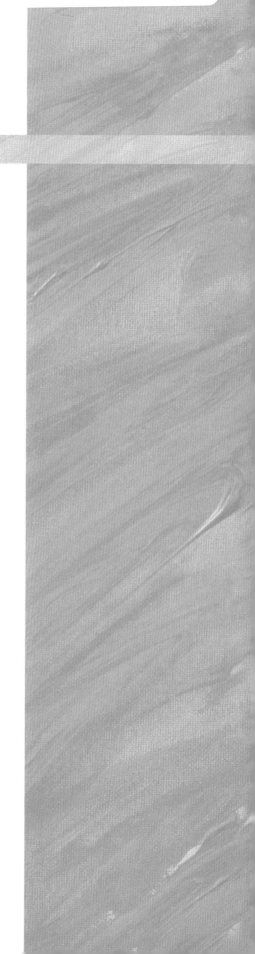

# Author Acknowledgments

*Make It Real: A Practical Resource for Teen-Friendly Evangelization* is very much a collective effort of many people over many years. I am grateful for the creativity, sense of humor, and insights of a host of gifted individuals.

I would like to particularly thank the staff of Cultivation Ministries, whose team effort truly made this book a reality. Specifically, I would like to thank Jennifer Kuhn for her invaluable support in this work. It was her contributions, editing, organizing, and cheerleading that made possible the completion of this book. I am grateful for the gaming expertise of Ela Mileska, the formatting of April Bailey, the creative and witty contributions of Karla Schrader, the incredible administrative organization of Michelle Kilbourne, the creative work of Casey Ross and Jenny Krumdick, and the always-encouraging office support of Diane Honeyman.

I am also grateful for the creative contributions of Becky and Eric Groth. I am proud to thank my oldest children (twins), Michael and Sarah Mercadante, for their creativity and sense of humor that are represented in these pages. I appreciate the practical testing and refining of this material by Pat Haviland and the Holy Cross peer ministry team of Batavia, Illinois.

I am very grateful for the soft editorial touch and wonderful editorial support of Laurie Delgatto of Saint Mary's Press.

Finally, I am grateful to my wife, Diane, and children, Sarah, Michael, Rebekah, Angela, Deborah, and Daniel. Thank you for your patience, kindness, and sacrifice that have helped make this book a reality.

For more information on youth ministry training, large-group evangelistic events, youth ministry resources, or opportunities for internships in large-event evangelization, please go to the Web site for Cultivation Ministries, *www.cultivationministries.com,* or contact us at *info@cultivationministries.com* or 630-513-8222.

CULTIVATION MINISTRIES
"Planting and Growing Effective Catholic Youth Ministries"

# Make It Real

## A Practical Resource
## for Teen-Friendly Evangelization

**Frank Mercadante**

Saint Mary's Press™

Genuine recycled paper with 10% post-consumer waste. Printed with soy-based ink. 5080500

The publishing team included Laurie Delgatto, development editor; Lorraine Kilmartin, consultant and reviewer; Mary M. Bambenek, administrator; Mary Koehler, permissions editor; Cheryl Drivdahl, copy editor; Barbara Bartelson, typesetter; Andy Palmer, art director; Kimberly K. Sonnek, designer; cover image, Digital Imagery copyright © by PhotoDisc, Inc.; manufacturing coordinated by the production services department of Saint Mary's Press.

Copyright © 2004 by Cultivation Ministries, P.O. Box 662, Saint Charles, IL 60174, www.cultivationministries.com. All rights reserved. Permission is granted to reproduce only the materials intended for distribution to the leaders and participants. No other part of this manual may be reproduced by any means without the written permission of the copyright holder.

Printed in the United States of America

Printing: 9 8 7 6 5 4 3 2 1

Year: 2012 11 10 09 08 07 06 05 04

ISBN 0-88489-817-2

Library of Congress Cataloging-in-Publication Data

Mercadante, Frank.
    Make it real : a practical resource for teen-friendly evangelization
/ Frank Mercadante.
        p. cm.
ISBN 0-88489-817-2 (pbk.)
    1. Church work with teenagers—Catholic Church.  I. Title.
BX2347 .8. Y7M475 2004
259'.23—dc22
                                                              2004007068

# Contents

## Part A:
## Setting the Foundation

## Part B:
## Evangelistic Outreach Sessions

# Part A
## Setting the Foundation

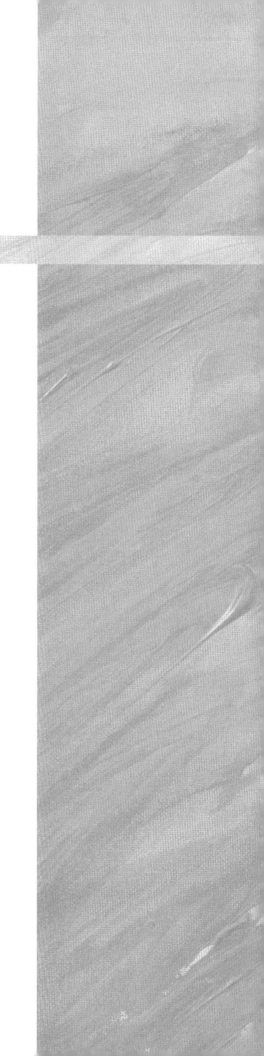

# What Is Evangelistic Outreach Programming?

## An Introduction to Evangelistic Outreach

While attending a "solemn" gathering of youth workers, I heard a requiem chorus gaining momentum. "Teens are too busy today," moaned a young, frustrated youth minister.

"They have no time for Church events," wailed a veteran youth ministry coordinator.

"Parents care more about their kids' sporting events than Church activities," grimly chimed another disillusioned youth worker.

And a litany of lamentations groaned on to the rhythm of the finely orchestrated dirge. I broke the beat by noting, "The problem isn't that teens are so busy that they don't have time for youth ministry offerings, as much as it is that those offerings are simply not worth their time."

Up to that point in my life, I had never considered dying as a martyr, let alone at the hands of Catholic youth ministers. But before the first stone could be chucked at my head, I quickly added: "Don't get me wrong: I agree—youth are busier than ever. I've often asked teens, 'Are you busy?' And without hesitation they almost always respond with a resounding, 'YES!' Today's teens have more opportunities than any other generation of young people. However, I will usually follow up with a second question: 'Are you so busy that you have no time to do the things you really want to do?' And with a knowing expression, they almost always concede that they find the time to do the things they really want to do. So, in other words, when we hear, 'I am too busy to attend youth ministry events,' it is a polite excuse for, 'Youth ministry is not worth my time.'"

Instead of focusing our efforts on building ministries that are truly worth teens' time, we have often shifted the blame onto our young people and their parents. We comfort ourselves by complaining, "If only they had their priorities right and were more committed to the Church." Additionally, we have combated their "complacency" by raising the age of Confirmation in order to conscript teens into our ministries. If they will not come on their own, we will make them come, we reason. Unfortunately, prisoners do not make great learners.

The best youth ministries stand on their own. Teens attend the events hosted by those ministries because they want to, and they want to because those events meet their needs. Young people invite their friends because they are proud of their Church and feel that it has something valuable to offer their peers.

I heartily agree with Jim Rayburn, the founder of Young Life, who said, "It's a sin to bore a kid with the Bible" (Young Life). When I first started in youth ministry, I wanted to construct a ministry that addressed the perceived needs of unevangelized teens. I wanted it to be a place where teens could have fun, develop friendships, hear the Good News in the light of their issues, and experience the love of Jesus Christ. I also sought to build a youth ministry where teens *wanted* to be, and to provide a "church" experience to which they were proud to invite their friends. Over the years I watched our ministry grow from about twelve teens to over three hundred on a given night. But more importantly, the ministry became a vehicle that the Holy Spirit used to touch many teens with the Good News of Jesus Christ.

## Defining Large-Group Evangelization

One of the most effective ways to reach a significant number of young people from a good cross-section of social groups is through large-group evangelization. *Large-group evangelization* can be defined as "consistent preaching of the Gospel to as many young people as possible through large-group gatherings that address perceived and unperceived needs of youth."

*Consistent* is a key part of the definition. A lack of consistency, or irregularity, is not only disturbing for the human digestive system; it also constipates the momentum of large-group evangelization. Large-group evangelization needs to be consistently planned for the same *day,* during the same *time,* at the same *location,* and with the same *quality* to have the maximum impact on teens' lives.

We are creatures of habit. Most days I have little recall of how I arrived at work. I know, of course, that I drove my car, but I remember little about making turns, stopping at lights, or going down streets. As a result of consistent repetition, I put very little thought into getting to work. (Some might say that is true about my approach to a lot of things!) Likewise, consistency in programming builds routine in young people's lives. Teens are very busy. Having to work at remembering a meeting lessens their chance of attending it. If they have to look at a calendar, find a schedule, or call a friend to find out where and when a gathering is, they are less likely to show up at it. Establishing the same day, time, and location for a recurring event reduces the amount of effort it takes to get to that event. Gatherings that are held every Sunday at 7:00 p.m. in the church gym are less likely to fall through the cracks of daily living than are sporadic events. Additionally, when we switch days, times, or locations, we have to publicize the event all over again.

A helpful trick is to name the event after the night it is held. For instance, you might call an event that is held every second Sunday of the month Second Sunday. If that name sounds too generic, try combining it with a catchy descriptive title, like Second Sunday Jam.

Young people are more apt to attend a gathering in a location that is familiar and comfortable. Teens who are not members of a parish might be hesitant to come to the parish church if they feel they do not belong there. That may not be a significant factor if teen members accompany most visitors to your youth events, but if your parish church is in a remote area, or if nonmembers are uncomfortable there for some reason, consider getting together at a more centralized, neutral, or well-known location.

Momentum, carried forth from one gathering to another, is an important dynamic of large-group evangelization. Large-group evangelization works optimally on a weekly or semi-monthly pattern. Monthly gatherings, though possibly effective in themselves, are too infrequent to reliably sustain momentum through the friction of daily life. Participants forget the fun, the relationships, and the impact.

Besides a consistent time and place, we need consistent high quality. Unfortunately, many young people presume that a church-sponsored event will be boring. That presumption is not the result of innate natural instincts; we youth ministers must concede that at times we have inadvertently formed it.

We have not always been known for our adventurous programming, innovation, or exciting sessions. Instead we have often served a steady diet of lifeless "teen" liturgies, meaningless meetings, and so-so, somber small groups! In many ways our gatherings have earned their reputation.

It should not be that way! Excellence should be our standard for ministry. Young people are surrounded by quality. We live in a fiercely competitive environment, and most institutions know that if they are to survive, they have to provide a superior service or product. Furthermore, young people today have a wide array of dazzling opportunities from which to choose. There are many different movies, TV channels, sporting events, and social activities, all competing for their time. If we are going to hold large-group evangelistic events, then we need to do them with "typical excellence" (with excellence so deeply ingrained in the events that it is considered part of their nature). If any message deserves to be presented with the highest standard of quality, it is the Good News of Jesus Christ. Teens expect us to apply ourselves and to make the things we plan for them worthwhile. We must put time into praying, planning, and preparing for our gatherings in order to make them creative and effective.

Teens live in a fairly closed environment. Word travels fast through their schools. Creating a positive and attractive image and reputation in the minds of young people is critical to the survival and growth of large-group gatherings. If youth ministry has a reputation for being boring, disorganized, and lifeless, we will sooner or later suffer extinction. We can produce a positive image by providing a gathering that is characterized by typical excellence.

## Large-Group Dynamics

A large-group evangelistic gathering characteristically involves twenty to several hundred teens. The dynamics of large groups differ from those of small groups. For instance, the wave, which is commonly enjoyed by large audiences at stadium gatherings, might look rather pathetic if attempted by eight teens in Mrs. Flemdrop's living room! Large-group evangelization is a unique form of programming, with its own personality, activities, patterns, and processes.

Before we look at the specifics of large-group dynamics, a word of caution: Because we plan a gathering for large numbers does not mean that hundreds of teens will necessarily attend. A gathering is not magical. Its size will be proportionate to our practice of relational youth ministry. Large-group evangelization gatherings become places for teens with whom we are building friendships. If both adult and teen leaders are invested in the program, are actively inviting newcomers, and are building relationships with the teens that attend, we will reap a great harvest. *Remember:* The foundation to successful large-group evangelization is the development of one-to-one relationships.

The large-group dynamic includes the following qualities: (1) opportunities to meet new people, (2) fast-paced and action-filled programming, (3) an enthusiastic tone, and (4) a message expressed through a variety of media. Let us look at each quality in detail.

### Opportunities to Meet New People

Most teens think it is fun to go places where a lot of other youth are present. Large-group evangelization capitalizes on that dynamic. It becomes part of the drawing card for a teen who may not necessarily be thinking about his relationship with God as much as about his crush on regular-attendee Drop Dead Darla. Getting to know Darla is a perceived need; getting to know Jesus Christ is a very real, but unperceived, need. Most unevangelized young people will attend events because of who will be there—not because of what will be presented.

Large-group events should be designed to help young people build friendships with one another. Teens will keep coming back to a program because they have made friends with other committed teens or have met adult leaders who care for them. We want to create a good and positive sense of interaction.

### Fast-Paced and Action-Filled Programming

Today's youth cut their teeth on television. They have been reared on *Sesame Street* and MTV, where scenes, camera angles, and perspectives change every few seconds. Consequently, many of today's adolescents have the attention span of a mosquito. Therefore, a large group of teens will lose interest quickly if programming stalls. Large-group programming should be fast paced and full of action. Most activities should last no more than 5–15 minutes. Any lull between activities will prove deadly; if we fail to immediately direct teens from one activity to the next, we will lose the group to side conversations. A night of wrestling the young people's attention back after each activity is exhausting for the leadership team and appears chaotic to the participants.

### An Enthusiastic Tone

Typically, young people have a lot of energy to burn. Most youth are not willing to sit for 2 hours on a hard floor listening to Dr. Sedation prove that even the most advanced insomniac is no match for his speaking skills. Something is wrong if teens are responding to our meetings with the same energy level as one suffering from carbon monoxide poisoning. Often, we, the leaders, are our own worst enemies when it comes to breeding a glacial climate. If we project reluctance and a lack of confidence in our programs, and explain activities with the enthusiasm of a backroom library clerk, our programs will surely suffer from low morale and attrition.

Attitudes are contagious. When I wake up in a negative mood, I often spread my poison to other family members. Next thing I know, we are all in a funk. Likewise, when I am in a positive mood, I often spread my exuberance to others. Large-group evangelistic meetings, therefore, must be carried out with enthusiasm. As leaders, we must set a standard. Activities should be introduced and led with high energy and excitement. Our attitude must emphatically proclaim, "It's great to be here!" Sooner or later, those attending will also feel positive and energized by the gatherings.

### A Message Expressed Through a Variety of Media

The large-group dynamic capitalizes on variety. Each teen has a different learning style. If we use an assortment of approaches, we increase our chances of touching the lives of a greater number of teens. Also, when gatherings become predictable, we know that we are in trouble. A variety of activities and media can keep our sessions fresh and lively: skits, dramas, mimes, interactive exercises, talks, witnesses, music, games, videos, slide shows, multimedia presentations, and so on. Variety for its own sake is not helpful. But when we use diverse media to shed light on a topic from different angles, we have a greater chance of holding the attention of the average teen. Activities should be carefully chosen to achieve the content objectives for the particular gathering, and should be sequenced in a purposeful and meaningful manner.

## More About Perceived and Unperceived Needs

We cannot hold to the "take your medicine" philosophy of youth ministry: "You know, it tastes bad, but it's good for you." On the other hand, we should not sugarcoat or water down the Gospel message in any way. Paul clearly cautions us against appealing to "tickling ears" (see 2 Timothy 2:2–44). Youth ministries that primarily entertain are not worth existing. Large-group evangelization at its best engages young people and earns their respect so that they are open to hearing the Gospel.

Effective large-group evangelization addresses both the *perceived* and the *unperceived* needs of young people. Many of those who came to Jesus did not arrive with spiritual conversion uppermost in their minds. They were seeking a more apparent need. They wanted to see because they were blind; they longed to walk because they were lame; they desired relief because they were hemorrhaging; they hoped for a miracle because a loved one was dying. Perceived needs fully absorbed their attention and moved them toward Jesus Christ. Once he met their perceived needs, they became open to addressing the very real, but unperceived, need for conversion.

I have found that many teens operate similarly. They are motivated primarily by a conscious need for fun, action, friendship, and interaction with members of the opposite sex. Ignoring those developmentally appropriate needs and leap-frogging to their spiritual needs is like preaching to a man who is dying of thirst. Gripped by the need for water, he is deaf to our "life-giving" message and turned off by our callous ignorance of that very obvious need. If we first address his thirst, we demonstrate that we truly care about him. Our message, in turn, becomes credible. With credibility comes a greater probability that he will return to us and seek our help with his spiritual needs.

Fruitful large-group evangelization enables teens to spend time with existing friends and to make new friends. In a culturally relevant manner, large-group evangelistic programming attempts to meet the perceived needs of teens by addressing common teenage issues such as loneliness, self-worth, peer pressure, stress, the future, friendship, family life, and dating in the light of the Scriptures and Church teaching, and attempts to meet the mostly unperceived needs of unevangelized teens by drawing them into a meaningful encounter with the person of Jesus Christ.

A common mistake made while developing a youth ministry is aiming to meet the needs of every level of spiritual maturity in a single, all-purpose large-group event. It is impossible to design a gathering that evangelizes new teens, fosters faith maturity in older teens, and equips teen leaders to minister to their peers. The "one-size-fits-all" event usually fails to meet any one need. Teens lose interest, and after a series of such gatherings, the entire program often defaults into a youth group that exists solely to meet its own needs.

The primary focus of large-group evangelistic programming is, as its title states, *evangelization.* The principal audience is active unconverted teens, inactive unevangelized teens, and unchurched teens. The gatherings are aimed at breaking down barriers that teens might have erected in their attitudes toward Jesus Christ and the Church, presenting the Gospel relevantly and in the light of contemporary teen issues, and inviting teens to a deeper relationship with the person Jesus Christ.

Though the content of large-group evangelistic programming is designed for unevangelized teens, that does not mean that already evangelized teens should opt out of attending the meetings that it generates. On the contrary, once young people's faith becomes personal and committed, we, as leaders, must pass on to them the importance of sharing their faith with others. Evangelized teens do not attend large-group events to address their own spiritual needs (there are other programs for that), but use the gatherings as an organized means of sharing their faith with their peers. If large-group evangelization is to be fruitful, teens with a growing faith must be committed to supporting the program by inviting their friends to be a part of their faith community and sharing their faith both interpersonally and programmatically. Large-group evangelistic gatherings multiply in attendance and spiritual impact when evangelized teens enthusiastically support the program's vision and purpose.

## Reaching Out to Many Teens

Large-group evangelization is designed for numerical growth—and more. Success in God's Reign is measured not by numbers but by the quality and quantity of spiritual fruit.

Therefore we have the responsibility to reach as many young people as possible, while keeping our focus on fruitfulness. The following questions serve as evaluative tools for outreach efforts.

### Are New People Coming?

A sign of life is that new people are regularly coming. If new teens are not attending our events, then we should ask why we are not attracting them. Are we providing an inviting and inclusive climate? Are we publicizing? Are the peer ministers inviting their friends? Do those attending know that they can invite their friends? Would they even want to invite their friends? Are we dealing with relevant issues in teens' lives? Are we holding gatherings on a night that is convenient? Are we praying? Conversely, if new teens are attending, we should ask what is attracting them.

### Are New People Returning?

Do teens attend once and never return? Do new teens feel welcome? Are they incorporated into the community? Do they feel like they are part of things? Are we following up on new teens in an organized manner? Or are they falling through administrative cracks? Are teens so unimpressed that they have no desire to return?

### Do Regulars Invite Their Friends?

Are regulars proud of the program and enthusiastic about including their friends? Is the program so enjoyable and fun that they want others to take part in it? Or are regulars reluctant to invite others? Do they perceive that their friends are welcome? Do they think that their friends will benefit from the gatherings? Do evangelized teens see the gatherings as events to which they can bring friends to hear the Gospel message and experience a sense of belonging?

### Are Regulars Returning?

Are we losing the regulars along the way? Are we still meeting their spiritual needs, or have they lost interest? Have we incorporated evangelized teens into programming that both fosters growth and meets their spiritual needs, and encouraged them to use large-group evangelization as an avenue for sharing their faith?

## A Meeting Format for Large-Group Evangelization

A large-group evangelistic gathering lasts from 1½ to 2 hours. It is planned and carried out in partnership with teen and adult leaders, and is divided into six movements that operate like steps in preparing a meal. As food must be defrosted, preheated, marinated, cooked, and sliced before it can be digested, so too must the content of a gathering be processed before it can be integrated. The six movements and their objectives are listed in the chart at the top of the next page and are explained in more detail in the text that follows the chart.

| Movement | Objective |
|---|---|
| 1. Pregathering hospitality | To create a warm and friendly environment |
| 2. Welcome | To help participants feel welcome |
| 3. Warm-up | To reduce discomfort and create openness |
| 4. Message | To communicate the Gospel message |
| 5. Closure | To wrap up the gathering |
| 6. Postgathering follow-up | To follow up on relationships |

### 1. Pregathering Hospitality (Defrost)

One afternoon a mother called my office. Her son attended our large-group evangelistic gatherings. She told me he had asked to be dropped off at least 5 minutes after the meetings started.

"Why is that?" I asked.

"He says that it's too painful to stand by himself before the meetings begin. No one talks with him or even acknowledges his presence. He could only look busy for so long by hanging out in the bathroom and by the drinking fountain. If he has to go, it would be easier for him to arrive late," she painfully disclosed to me.

My heart sank. I wondered how many other teens had had the same experience as her son's. At that moment I decided to make some very intentional efforts to change the atmosphere at our gatherings. There was no excuse for a teen to feel unwelcome, uncomfortable, or alone among a group who were supposed to be known for their love for one another (see John 13:35).

Providing a hospitable climate is absolutely essential to being effective in reaching out to teens. As the saying goes, "You don't get a second chance to make a first impression." If a young person feels insignificant, unwelcome, or unnoticed, there is little chance that she or he will return.

The impact of a warm, accepting, and hospitable atmosphere cannot be underestimated in its power to attract and hold the participation of teens.

A hospitable climate does not come naturally. As a matter of fact, hospitality is often quite unnatural. What are customary are cliques and exclusive groups. We are naturally attracted to the people we know. To be a welcoming group requires constant attentive effort on the part of the leaders. We must consistently sacrifice our own comfort for the well-being of our participants. Leaders' huddling contentedly together at the start of a meeting is a cultural taboo for large-group evangelization.

Stationing leaders at the door to the meeting room, to enthusiastically greet teens as they arrive, helps to ensure that young people feel welcome as soon as they walk in. We should make contact with each young person before the gathering ever begins. We can create a positive and warm atmosphere by playing some upbeat contemporary Catholic music in the background. Additionally, several leaders should be "hospitable roamers," that is, wanderers on the lookout for teens who are standing alone or looking out of place.

Pregathering hospitality usually begins with a team prayer about 15 minutes before the meeting. We should complete all preparations and setup at least 20 minutes before the start of the gathering so that after the prayer, we can give our full attention to the teens' arrival.

### 2. Welcome (Preheat)

Most people walk in the door of a meeting room stiff and uncomfortable—like a cold lawnmower. A grass cutter's engine will not roar unless the carburetor is properly primed. Likewise, the participants need to be primed by being made to feel comfortable and welcome. Pregathering hospitality sets the climate; the welcome phase officially begins the gathering. The purpose of this movement is to foster a sense of familiarity and ease in those present. It gives participants an opportunity to meet and interact with other people in the room, and therefore reduces the tension associated with unfamiliarity. Activities in this phase might include these:

- An enthusiastic welcome and opening comments
- An opening prayer
- Identification of newcomers and an official welcome for them
- Videos or computer slide shows of participants from past meetings
- Mixers that get the teens interacting with one another
- Fun music or songs with actions, that compel people to move around

- Introductory skits or dramas that make people laugh (Make sure that these do not make fun of, potentially humiliate, or embarrass any young person; that would be anything but welcoming.)
- Activities that help young people feel welcome and a part of the group

The welcoming phase usually lasts from 10 to 20 minutes. It builds off the informal warmth of the pregathering hospitality phase and leads to the warm-up phase.

### 3. Warm-Up (Marinate)

The objective of the warm-up phase is to continue fostering a sense of familiarity, have some fun, burn off energy, and prepare the teens for the message. Warm-up can last anywhere from 15 to 30 minutes. It often consists of games, icebreakers, funny skits, relays, or fun songs—and it is all the better if those activities relate to the topic of the gathering.

We should choose games and activities that fit the personality of the teens in our community. Some groups are wild and crazy and enjoy games that fit the same description. Other groups are sophisticated and stick their noses in the air when asked to play "silly, childish" games.

A good game is both fun to play and enjoyable to watch. Games should be carefully planned and tried out before hand. We should articulate the directions clearly, provide concrete examples, and possibly play a practice round so that our audience is not left confused. It is essential to consider safety and emotional issues: we cannot play games that put teens at risk of serious injury or of embarrassment. The warm-up phase should be fun for everyone and should successfully lead the group to a greater receptivity of the message phase.

### 4. Message (Cook)

During the message phase, we creatively communicate the good news of God's Reign—not our own personal message. Our presentation must reflect God's transforming word as revealed through the Scriptures and Church teaching. The message should be planned prayerfully (providing a great focus for our intercessory prayer team, as explained in chapter 2), designed in a developmentally appropriate manner, expressed creatively and relevantly, and situated within the common experiences and issues that teens face.

The message can be communicated through many different media and activities that build on one another. (We should consider including the media and activities listed in resource 1, "A Large-Group Evangelization Planner.")

The message phase should be a good mix of presentation, reflection, and small-group interaction. The large group can be divided into small discussion teams led by adults or teens, or both. Even though the tempo of the gathering slows down during the message phase, avoid activities that keep the teens sitting for long periods of time. Our minds can absorb only what our bodies can endure. The message should be presented in an experiential manner and should include an opportunity for the teens to respond.

### 5. Closure (Slice)

The last movement in the organized gathering is closure. It includes a basic summary of the main points of the message, which can be expressed in a simple verbal statement or through a skit, a song, or a slide show. It can take place through a closing prayer service.

Closure may also include an evangelistic invitation—that is, an invitation to respond to the call of Jesus Christ, or to act on the message. Invitation involves moving the teens from hearing about Jesus Christ, to opening the doors to their hearts and experiencing him personally. The following is an example of an evangelistic invitation:

> Tonight we learned the four characteristics of being a great friend; hopefully, we can apply them to our friendships and become better friends to others. We also learned that Jesus Christ is the perfect example of those four characteristics. Jesus Christ is the ultimate friend. He is the kind of friend we all need. How would you rate your friendship with him? Is he just a name, not a person you really know? Is he a distant acquaintance? Is he an occasional friend? Whatever status Jesus Christ holds in your life today, he is inviting you to more. He is the friend of friends, who invites you to a deeper relationship with him. In the Book of Revelation, Jesus says: "Behold, I stand at the door and knock. If anyone hears my voice and opens the door, [then] I will enter his house and dine with him, and he with me" (3:20). Jesus is inviting us to intimacy. If you desire that intimacy and want to pray for Jesus Christ to become your closest friend, then pray with me tonight.

### 6. Postgathering Follow-Up (Digest)

After the gathering, we do not want the teens stampeding toward the door in a wild frenzy to escape. It is to be hoped that our atmosphere, message, and community life will influence the teens to stick around a few minutes after the planned programming ends; the best stuff usually happens following the structured gathering. We should leave the last 10–15 minutes of scheduled time for follow-up interaction, and provide some simple and inexpensive refreshments to motivate the teens to stick around. (It is a well-known, scientific fact that teens are always hungry.) During this time we can continue to develop relationships with the teens. We can also get more personally involved in their lives with questions such as, "What did you think about the message this evening?" We should be open to any interpersonal evangelization opportunities that present themselves after the gathering.

Additionally, we can include some formal follow-up by arranging a short meeting with young people who responded to an evangelistic invitation. At that meeting we can distribute materials or resources, and perhaps also ask the teens to sign up for a small group that could help foster further growth in their faith.

## Steps in Planning a Large-Group Gathering

A large-group gathering should be planned in a spirit of prayer. We should always seek the Holy Spirit's particular guidance on behalf of the teens we are seeking to reach. The following steps can help us do so. Chapters 5–10 present six sessions arranged around these steps; resource 1 can be used to develop other evangelization gatherings.

### 1. Determine the Topic

The topic or theme for a gathering should be prayerfully discerned. Subjects should be based on real teen issues. We might surface ideas through a needs assessment, a program evaluation, or a brainstorming session with teens. Choosing topics for an entire year will give us time to gather ideas and resources well in advance of the individual gatherings.

Teens build resistance to some topics. They may grimace if we say, for example, "Next week's topic is self-worth." Does that mean they have mastered the theme of self-image and have no further need to hear about it? Absolutely not! The issue is most certainly relevant, but the topic title has gotten old and overused. To avoid such negative reactions, topics should be publicized using creative titles. For instance, a gathering that addresses our common misconceptions of God might be titled "God: Mirage or Real Deal."

## 2. Formulate Objectives

To convey our content effectively, we must first state specifically what we hope to achieve through it. Like our topic, our objectives should be discerned prayerfully and rooted in the Scriptures and in Church teaching. They should be evangelistic in scope, and stated in terms of what we hope the participants will come to value (affective), know (cognitive), or do (behavioral). We must be cautious not to cover too much in one sitting. It is best to keep it simple. One to three content objectives are realistic.

## 3. Pool Resources

Once we know what we are trying to accomplish, we can consider how to do it. Pooling resources provides a range of options. This stage involves brainstorming for new ideas; examining books, programs, and catalogs for appropriate materials; and networking with other youth workers to share creativity and experience. We must be sure to consider good Catholic resources so that we will be able to present the message in a genuinely Catholic manner. Depending on our situation, we may create new material from scratch, or pull scripts, learning activities, or videos from published sources. Even the most creative groups experience blocks or time crunches. Therefore, it is important to develop a library of youth ministry resources to support our efforts.

## 4. Choose Activities

While pooling resources, we may have identified two outside speakers, a video presentation, three topical discussion sheets, a teen willing to give a witness talk, a couple of good songs, three skits, and a learning activity. Our next step is to narrow down the options to those that best help us achieve our objectives. We may discard some ideas because they do not fit the objectives, they are not financially feasible, we are short on time, we do not have the expertise that they require, or they duplicate an earlier activity. We should pick the activities that are best suited for the objectives and circumstances.

## 5. Sequence Activities

The effectiveness of what we do depends on the order in which we do it. Activities must be placed in the proper sequence if the gathering is to progress intelligently and meaningfully. For example, using a powerfully emotional skit might put the teens in a mood that prohibits further discussion or movement. Or, if they were not prepared for the skit, it might have little impact. Or, if the previous activity was lighthearted, it might be mistaken as funny.

Good sequencing generally begins by introducing the topic in a nonthreatening manner. An upbeat introduction can be provided by a skit or a story that illustrates the theme, or by a video that records teens' comments about the topic. The introduction might be followed up with a small-group discussion that allows the teens to share their experience with the topic. Next might come something driven a little more by content, like a witness talk by a peer minister; then a powerful video; and finally, a closing prayer service. Proper sequencing usually begins with a lighthearted mood and a general focus and application, and progressively moves to a more intense mood, a more detailed focus, and a deeper personal application.

### 6. Assign Responsibilities

Once the activities have been chosen and sequenced, it is time to assign responsibilities. We should break the gathering down into smaller action steps and detail who will do what by when. Then we can follow up with one another to ensure that everything is completed on time.

### 7. Implement Plans

The implementation step moves the gathering from paper to reality. We begin the event by praying for each person involved and each activity scheduled. Then we ought to follow the plan for the gathering, yet not be afraid to adapt things according to changing circumstances or the prompting of the Holy Spirit.

### 8. Evaluate

At the end of the session or at the next leadership meeting, we should take a few minutes to evaluate the event. Evaluation makes us vulnerable and at times can be painful. However, the long-term result is progressive growth and further excellence in programming.

We must always keep an ear open to what teens think about our gatherings. We can talk with them after the events, and periodically invite them to do formal, written evaluations.

## Conclusion

If we desire to move forward acres at a time in our efforts to evangelize teenagers, we need to present them with "food" that is digestible. We will lose them indefinitely and do the cause of Catholicism a major injustice if we bore them with the greatest message humanity has ever received and known.

Large-group evangelization achieves optimum results if it becomes an established, regular, weekly or semimonthly event, occurring at the same time and location, with consistent quality. It is important to build momentum in ministry and to help teens form attendance habits. The event should have a catchy name, and excellence in programming ought to be the norm. A variety of innovative and creative tools and media should be used to share the Good News. Such a large-group approach has a dynamic that allows teens to meet new people, experience a fast-paced program, and tap into a contagious enthusiasm.

As ministers, and in the footsteps of our Lord, we must strategically meet the perceived and unperceived needs of our teens. Large-group gatherings must have an evangelistic purpose, and leaders should use such gatherings as stepping-stones to relational ministry with the teens who attend. Large-group events are designed to reach out to as many teenagers as possible. However, numerical growth should be sought not simply for its own sake but rather for bringing as many into Christ's fold as possible.

Effective formats for large-group gatherings typically include six phases: pregathering hospitality, welcome, warm-up, message, closure, and postgathering follow-up. Determining the topic, formulating objectives, pooling resources, choosing activities, sequencing events, assigning responsibilities, implementing plans, and evaluating outcomes are all necessary steps in planning such a gathering.

(Much of this chapter is adapted from Frank Mercadante, *Growing Teen Disciples,* chap. 8.)

# A Large-Group Evangelization Planner

## Planning Steps

1. Determine the topic
2. Formulate objectives
3. Pool resources
4. Choose activities
5. Sequence activities
6. Assign responsibilities
7. Implement plans
8. Evaluate

## Objective Types

1. Affective
2. Cognitive
3. Behavioral

## Meeting Movements

1. Pregathering hospitality
2. Welcome
3. Warm-up
4. Message
5. Closure
6. Postgathering follow up

## Activity Formats

| | | |
|---|---|---|
| Introduction | Small-group discussion | Live music |
| Icebreaker | Reflection | Recorded music |
| Large-group mixer | Mime | Case study |
| Small-group mixer | Shadow mime | Story |
| Large-group game | Skit | Scripture reading |
| Small-group game | Role-play | Witness talk |
| Competitive game | Video | Keynote presentation |
| Simulation | Slide show | Theme exercise |
| Large-group discussion | Multimedia presentation | |

  **Resource 1:** Permission to reproduce is granted. © 2004 by Cultivation Ministries.

## Meeting Schedule

**Program Title:** _____   **Date:** _____   **Theme:** _____

| Time | Meeting Movement | Activity | Objective | Person Responsible |
|------|------------------|----------|-----------|--------------------|
| 6:45 | | | | |
| 6:50 | | | | |
| 6:55 | | | | |
| 7:00 | | | | |
| 7:05 | | | | |
| 7:10 | | | | |
| 7:15 | | | | |
| 7:20 | | | | |
| 7:25 | | | | |
| 7:30 | | | | |
| 7:35 | | | | |
| 7:40 | | | | |
| 7:45 | | | | |
| 7:50 | | | | |
| 7:55 | | | | |
| 8:00 | | | | |
| 8:05 | | | | |
| 8:10 | | | | |
| 8:15 | | | | |
| 8:20 | | | | |
| 8:25 | | | | |
| 8:30 | | | | |
| 8:35 | | | | |
| 8:40 | | | | |
| 8:45 | | | | |
| 8:50 | | | | |
| 8:55 | | | | |
| 9:00 | | | | |
| 9:05 | | | | |
| 9:10 | | | | |
| 9:15 | | | | |

# Chapter Two

## The Heartbeat of Evangelistic Outreach

### Essential Dynamics for Success

When my children were young, Christmas morning was highly anticipated. Discovering under the tree an item they had requested from Santa brought bright grins and wide eyes. Watching their animated expressions while they opened their gifts was one of the true joys of parenthood.

One year my wife and I bought an electric racetrack that was item number one on our son Daniel's Christmas list. Daniel was particularly thrilled with this gift, and I found myself quickly assembling the track, guardrails, and car decals for him. As soon as everything was ready to go, I attempted to plug the transformer into an electrical outlet. With the controls tightly gripped in his fingers, Daniel just could not wait to start racing. To my surprise, I discovered that the track was powered not through an electrical outlet but by batteries. Unaware of that, I had not purchased any batteries, nor did I have any extras around the house. Daniel's amazement soon disintegrated into despair when he realized that the wonderful gift Santa had brought him would not work without batteries. We just stared in disappointment at our fully assembled, but totally powerless, track.

Daniel's experience differs little from that of enthusiastic youth workers who purchase the latest groundbreaking resource for youth ministry. After scrupulously following the script and enacting the program, they realize that there is no power on the pages or magic in the ink. For most youth leaders, one of the hardest lessons to learn is that the spiritual current that powers an evangelistic impact cannot be programmed or packaged. Somehow, we have a hard time accepting that there is no programmatic panacea.

If the program content in this book (and others) cannot ignite a young person's heart, what can? What impacts a young person's life? What animates an evangelistic ministry? What activates an event?

## Evangelistic Intercession

Intercessory prayer is the first nonnegotiable element of evangelistic youth ministry. Intercession is far too important to be considered an "if we have some time at the end" activity. If we want to see lives supernaturally transformed, we had best invest in prayer. Too often we underestimate the power of prayer and underschedule it as a nonessential activity. The simple fact is, prayer has the power to change people, programs, and ultimately history.

While preparing for an evangelistic retreat, Diane, one of our teen leaders, came to me and said: "After praying, I think God wants my friend Kara to go on this retreat. I asked her, but she said no because she was starting her new job on that weekend. But, I still think she is supposed to go."

I really did not know how to respond, so I motioned for her to sit down and I asked if we could pray for her friend. I was mostly offering to pray with her so that she could put her dilemma to rest. While praying, however, I was overcome with the same conviction. I cannot explain it, but I also knew that God wanted Kara to go on that retreat. Diane and I agreed that we would pray every day for Kara—that somehow the Lord would open the door for her to attend.

We prayed fervently for over two weeks with no results. Then, two days before the retreat, Kara unexpectedly called me at home. She said: "Funny thing happened. My new boss called me this evening and asked if I could delay my starting day until next weekend. I was wondering if I could still attend that retreat?"

Before she could finish, I yelled: "Yes! Of course you can come!"

Kara attended the retreat and heard all about God's love for her. The Lord had inspired Diane and me to pray for Kara and had answered our prayer in a convincing manner. But the true significance of that prayer was not made clear until six months later when Kara tragically died in a motorcycle accident. The Lord had wanted Kara to understand his love for her before she left this earth.

Prayer is powerful, and placing it as a priority in our lives and ministries must become our operating paradigm. We often do not have enough time to do everything that needs to be done. So we prefer to expend our energy on activities that we can measure—planning a meeting, creating a flier, choosing an icebreaker, and so on. And we genuinely feel good when we accomplish something we view as practical and useful.

Jesus clearly viewed prayer as essential, practical, and active. He said: "Ask, and it will be given to you; seek and you will find; knock and the door will be opened to you. For everyone who asks, receives; and the one who seeks, finds; and to the one who knocks, the door will be opened" (Matthew 7:7–8). Prayer simply works. Because evangelization is primarily the work of the Holy Spirit, prayer must be at the center of every evangelistic activity. It is the unseen, but very real, power that makes evangelization truly forceful and life changing.

### Practical Suggestions

Too often we only mentally affirm the priority and power of prayer. Our convictions need to be transformed into commitments. The following practical suggestions can help you create a powerful base for intercessory prayer:

- Gather an intercessory team in the room where a meeting will take place. Invite the team to do these things:
  - Pray over each chair that a teen will later occupy.
  - Pray by the doors to the room, asking the Holy Spirit to touch each person who enters and exits.
  - Sprinkle holy water in the room to consecrate it for God's purposes.
- Give each team leader a list of the young people on her or his team. Ask the leaders to pray for each team member regularly, and especially before program sessions.
- Ask a group of older people to pray for individual young people or for the youth ministry team, or for both, daily.
- Ask a group of intercessors to follow a gathering's schedule (in real time) and pray for the desired outcome for each activity. They can do so either on- or off-site.
- Include intentions about a youth event in the prayers of the faithful during the liturgy on the Sunday before the event.
- Before a meeting pray for or over those who will be bringing the message by giving talks, witnessing, performing skits, acting in dramas, and so forth.
- Develop a monthly prayer calendar that includes prayer requests pertaining to youth ministry for each day of the month. Incorporate specific requests for each evangelistic outreach event.

• Before planning any evangelistic outreach event, spend an extended time praying for God's guidance and direction.

## An Evangelistic Climate

After weeks of gentle nudging and positive encouragement, Dominic's mother finally convinced him to give their parish youth ministry a shot. Dominic was typical of many teens: he did not think he would know anyone involved, and he figured the gatherings would be boring. But Dominic's mother reasoned that if she could just get him to one meeting, Dominic would probably like it and return in the future. Unfortunately, the experience of that one meeting only hardened Dominic's resolve to avoid the program.

Dominic was dropped off at the parish door. As he walked into the meeting room, he recognized some not-so-friendly faces from school. It seemed that everyone was preoccupied with his or her own agenda and failed to notice him. Those few minutes before the meeting seemed like endless hours as Dominic stood awkwardly alone, embarrassed and angry. There was nothing positive about feeling unwelcome and insignificant. Not surprisingly, Dominic never went back to his parish's youth ministry.

Central to any youth evangelization program is a positive, warm, and inviting climate. The vast majority of teens will evaluate the worth of a meeting primarily on how welcomed, cared for, or accepted they feel. The most powerful evangelistic messages will fall on deaf ears if the atmosphere contradicts their basis in love.

The best evangelization programs proclaim the Gospel concretely through Christian hospitality. To operate with integrity, we must make great efforts to truly welcome and love every teen who walks through our doors, *especially* the "stranger." Hospitality cannot be an afterthought or left to spontaneity; it must be planned and intentional, and those responsible for extending it must be held accountable. The reason is that hospitality does not come naturally to all of us. What does come naturally for most of us is gravitating toward those we know. For adults, but especially for teens, cliques naturally evolve from comfortable relationships. It takes real effort to leave our cliques behind and pursue a conversation with someone we do not know. To do that we have to abandon our comfort zone and overcome the awkwardness of meeting a stranger.

We like to be with people who love and value us. Therefore, an atmosphere of love is the second nonnegotiable component of an evangelistic outreach program. Great pains should be taken to provide a genuinely caring and accepting environment.

In fact, in John 13:35, Jesus says that others will identify us as his disciples because of our "love for one another." In other words, we are called to build a reputation of love. It should be nothing more than ordinary for a visitor at a youth outreach event to comment, "The people here really make me feel loved." If we are not consistently hearing that people find a special sense of love and a welcome in our hospitable environment, then we are probably not living up to our bottom-line call as followers of Jesus Christ. "Love for one another" is our trademark, our niche in the world, the heart and soul of a true community of disciples.

Besides being welcoming and loving, our evangelistic outreach environment should be different from anything else our teens have experienced. The atmosphere we establish should communicate unconditional acceptance and should encourage teens to be themselves. Many environments created for teens are nothing more than costume parties that they can enter safely only if they wear masks concealing their true identities. Young people long for a place where they can take off their masks and be real without penalty.

To achieve the exceptional hospitality that we are looking for, we must first build a culture of care among the members of our youth ministry team. The process of doing that begins when the adult leaders start to answer the call to love others as if it were a direct order from God (which it is!). If we want to build genuine community among the teen participants, we must first model it among the adult leaders.

We must then transfer the value of loving one another to the hearts of our teen leaders. We must constantly reinforce the message verbally. We must evaluate the effectiveness of our hospitality and hold ourselves accountable to an established standard. Finally, we must set in place some practical expressions that make our love and care tangible so that the teens attending our meetings experience them.

## Practical Suggestions

Again, understanding the importance of developing a hospitable climate is not enough. The following practical suggestions can help you move from conviction to reality:

- Assign several adult and youth leaders to sincerely welcome and greet teen members and guests at the door. Assign a second group of leaders to stay in the meeting room to further welcome and get to know them, especially looking out for any teen standing alone.
- Personally call or write to thank teens after they attend their first gathering. Include an invitation to the next meeting.
- Develop a set of "guarantees" that every teen walking through the door is entitled to experience. Those guarantees should specify how the team will make guests feel welcome and loved. For example: "No one will ever stand alone without anybody to talk to for more than 5 seconds before a member of our hospitality team approaches him or her in a friendly manner" or "We will take a photograph of every first timer at the meeting, and send it to that person with a note on the back that says, 'Thanks for spending last Sunday with us!'" (See resource 2, "Good News Guaranteed," for a chart that your team can use in developing its own guarantees.)
- Provide adult and teen leaders with training on welcoming, initiating conversation, and listening. Make it a meeting taboo for any three teen leaders to be talking together without the company of at least one teen participant.
- Help develop an environment where teens are accepted for who they are. Train your leaders to be open and accepting of others (both verbally and nonverbally). Create a "no-mask" zone, where your leaders model authenticity.
- Evaluate every gathering with the question, "Did we welcome and treat everyone in a manner that left people thinking, 'I can tell they are disciples of Jesus Christ by the way they love'?"

## An Encounter with Jesus Christ

Once we have prepared for our outreach in prayer and established a loving climate, then we have laid a firm foundation on which to build. But what exactly are we seeking to build? Evangelization is not about big numbers or Hollywood-like productions. At the heart of any evangelistic effort is the drawing of teens into a life-changing encounter with the person Jesus Christ. We certainly should seek to be relevant, to attract as many teens as possible, and to conduct our sessions with the kind of excellence that befits the dignity of the Gospel. However, the only purpose behind relevancy, growing numbers, and excellent events is to bring young people into a relationship with the risen Lord.

Most teens are not necessarily looking to be involved in religious institutions, nor are they particularly trusting of organized religion. They are, however, hungering for an experience of God. Event evangelization ought to create the conditions necessary for that experience to occur. Large-group evangelization is invitational. At the center of its message is the call to meet Jesus Christ—the great lover of souls.

Teens need to be invited into a relationship with Jesus Christ (and, of course, with the community of his disciples) both programmatically and interpersonally. Programming should always lead young people into a deeper relationship with Jesus Christ. Whether the topic is conformity, loneliness, or even dating, the focal point should be Jesus Christ. We should invite teens to cling to Jesus Christ, the rock, while peeling off the grip of peer pressure; to grab the hand of Jesus Christ, the true friend, while sinking in the quicksand of loneliness; and to allow Jesus Christ to be their navigator while exploring the uncharted roads of a new dating relationship. Additionally, we should offer prayer or worship experiences that support our message and that place teens in the presence of God.

An evangelization program that is only invitational is incomplete; to be effective it must also be personal. Both adult and teen leaders must be motivated and skilled in the art of interpersonal evangelization and should follow up the program's content with individual participants.

There are several ways that adult and teen leaders can continue the work of evangelization after a meeting. At the actual event, we can set aside time for participants and team members to mingle (recall that this is the postgathering follow-up, or digest, stage). Adult and teen leaders should talk with teen participants about what the participants heard and how they are responding to it. This is a time particularly suited for listening; often teens will raise questions or practical implications that the meeting format was unable to address in a personal manner. This is also a good time to share one's own story of how Jesus Christ has given direction, support, and guidance in regard to the program topic. Opportunities to pray for or with teens may arise naturally in response to the message.

Failing to support the programmatic expression of evangelization with an interpersonal expression often leads to a

"Christian when in church" mentality. If teens see Christianity lived solely within the safety of programs, and not addressed in real life by real people, they will dichotomize their expression of faith: while in church they will put on their religious hat, and in real life they will take it off. Programming should support real-life interpersonal evangelization, and not vice versa.

It is important to note that while youth evangelization is centrally about leading teens into a relationship with Jesus Christ, it is always presented within the context of community. As Catholics we do not endorse only a "me and Jesus Christ" approach to living our faith. We are evangelized into a community of believers who help give expression, support, and accountability to our faith. If Jesus had been concerned only about our loving God, he would not have given us a second commandment to love others.

### Practical Suggestions

The following practical suggestions can help you move from just talking about Jesus Christ to fostering an encounter with him:

- Include verbal invitations during the message or closure section of a meeting. For example, during a session about loneliness, say: "We are relational people. We were created with a desire to share our lives, thoughts, dreams, and fears with others. But there are times when we feel bottled up, alone and isolated. We may even be surrounded by 'friends,' and be going to all the right parties with all the right people, yet still feel alone. But the reality is that we are not alone. We have a friend who is always with us. We have a friend who loves us more than we could ever imagine. That friend is Jesus Christ, and he is calling your name. He says, 'I will never forsake you or abandon you' (Hebrews 13:5). The prophet Isaiah spoke of God's love for us in this way: 'Can a mother forget her infant, be without tenderness for the child of her womb? Even should she forget, I will never forget you. See, upon the palms of my hands I have written your name' (Isaiah 49:15–16)."
- Toward the end of the meeting, integrate a time for personal reflection. Summarize the message by saying something like this: "Jesus Christ addresses the greatest hungers of our hearts. We were designed to be in relationship with him. Where are you in your relationship with Jesus Christ? Who is he in your life?" Then create a time for reflection by playing instrumental music. Follow up by leading the teens

in a prayer response that focuses on making Jesus Christ the center of their lives. Offer practical suggestions about how to grow in a relationship with Jesus Christ beyond the meeting. Include the recommendation that they share with one other person the commitment to make Jesus Christ the center of their lives.

- Close the meeting with an opportunity to receive the sacrament of Penance and Reconciliation. This can take the form of a communal reconciliation service or individual reconciliation.
- Close the meeting with a prayer service that centers on responding to the primary message of the session. The service may be based on ritual or may be more spontaneous. The key is to bring the young people into a real prayer experience, and not simply lead them through the motions.
- Close the meeting with prayer and worship, using songs that address the topic or that call forth a response to Jesus Christ. Arrange for a music ministry group or a cantor to facilitate this closing.

## A Relational Ministry

Many of us grew up during a time when most of our contact with youth leaders and catechists took place in organized and formal programs. Rarely did we interact with those adults outside the church environment. Consequently, we did not get to know them very well. Additionally, our meetings tended to be driven by content. We learned what we needed to know about being Catholic, but we failed to learn how to get to know one another.

Faith is best passed on from person to person, not from program to person. If a program makes a difference in our lives, it usually does so as a result of our relationships with the people involved in it.

Relational youth ministry is, essentially, entering the lives of teens. It means things like calling teens between youth gatherings, attending their athletic events, meeting small groups of them at fast-food restaurants, and writing notes or sending cards. (Practical relational ministry must be carried out prudently and in accord with individual parish and diocesan guidelines.) The point is that relational ministry extends evangelization beyond the church meeting room and into the drama of real life. Evangelization is not exclusively the task of the program but also the interpersonal work of each youth ministry leader.

The best youth ministries provide dual evangelistic support, through excellent programming and an expansive web of meaningful relationships. Teens are confident and proud to bring their friends to a meeting. They are certain that their friends will be greeted with warmth, treated hospitably, and included in the community. They know that the Gospel message will be proclaimed in a relevant and creative manner. They expect that the content of the session will give them plenty to talk with their friends about afterward, leading to the interpersonal aspect of evangelization. Additionally, they know that the leaders will take an interest in the friends they bring and will support their evangelistic efforts.

Jesus illustrated that dualistic approach in his own ministry. The Incarnation itself is an expression of relational ministry. God became human, entered our world, and journeyed with us. Furthermore, Jesus did not simply address large crowds or work exclusively through synagogue services, but shared the Gospel interpersonally with individuals such as Nicodemus, Martha, the rich young ruler, and the woman at the well. So must we.

## Practical Suggestions

Again, understanding the importance of developing a relational approach to ministry is not enough. The following practical suggestions can help you move from conviction to reality:

- Build into your leadership training programming a component that introduces a relational paradigm for youth ministry and the tools to be successful.
- Develop clear expectations that leaders will reach out to teens beyond the program.
- Encourage leaders to make at least one contact each week with a teen outside the youth gathering. A phone call, a note, an e-mail, a personal meeting, or attendance at a school event (such as a choir concert or a wrestling match) are examples. (Again, keep in mind appropriate parish and diocesan guidelines.)
- Discuss the relational aspect of ministry during your leadership meetings. Encourage people to share what they are doing to build relationships with teens.
- Give your leaders birthday cards, addressed envelopes, stamps, and their teen members' birth dates. Ask each leader to write personal notes and to send the cards before their participants' birthdays. You might even suggest writing notes to celebrate the teens' Baptism anniversaries. Having

the supplies available makes the task much easier for busy leaders.

- Divide the teen participants into small teams that gather for a portion of each meeting (any friends brought by members belong to those members' teams). Assign adult and youth leaders to each team, and explain that their role includes regular (outside-the-meeting) contact with the individual members of the team.
- Have the leaders regularly look in local papers for articles about teens who are involved in your youth ministry program. Ask the leaders to cut out the articles and send them with congratulatory notes to the teens.

## Conclusion

Effective evangelization cannot be purchased in a book or packaged in a program. The best resources can default into a programming "code blue" if the leadership fails to pay attention to "heartbeat" dynamics. Underneath the surface of any life-changing evangelistic youth ministry are essential elements that animate the shell. Paying careful attention to prayerful intercession, building a loving and accepting environment, offering opportunities to encounter Jesus Christ personally and meaningfully, and undergirding every program with a web of significant relationships offers life to any evangelistic effort.

# Good News Guaranteed

The following statements are guarantees that we, as a team, are pledging to any teens who come to one of our large-group meetings. These guarantees will help us lovingly demonstrate the Good News to any young person who frequents our gatherings. The strategy we will use to accomplish each guarantee and the steps we will take to carry out that strategy are also listed here.

**GUARANTEE No. ___**

## Strategy

| No. | Strategy Step |
|-----|---------------|
|     |               |
|     |               |
|     |               |
|     |               |
|     |               |

**GUARANTEE No. ___**

## Strategy

| No. | Strategy Step |
|-----|---------------|
|     |               |
|     |               |
|     |               |
|     |               |
|     |               |

# Chapter Three

## Multiplying the Yield

### Growing an Outreach Program by Paying Attention to the Little Things

As a parish youth minister, I was involved in a large-group evangelistic ministry called Advance! The gatherings steadily grew, until about three hundred teens attended. As a result the ministry attracted the attention of many youth ministers in the area. Often similar programs sprang up in nearby parishes, some of them even possessing the same name. Imitation is certainly a form of flattery, but in most cases the other ministries did not achieve the hoped-for results.

That scenario is common. Why? Although we are able to learn from the experiences, wisdom, and programs of other youth ministers and ministries, I believe that the effectiveness of those others has to do with some subtle nuances, or intangibles, that are often not addressed in attempts at replication. This chapter discusses some of the practical intangibles that make all the difference when trying to attract teens to a parish youth ministry and keep them involved in it.

### Building the Right Tone

Occasionally I shop for clothing with my teenage children. Flitting in and out of a variety of establishments that cater to teens is an education in contrasts. Not only does each store carry a certain style or feel in clothing, but each also has its own environment and culture. There are a tone, an emotion, and a sense that you develop when you walk in the door. Some places are genuinely friendly and centered on the customer. Others are just the opposite. One store in particular seems to revel in being snobbish, positioning its clothing as the attire of the elite. Instead of being warm and helpful, the clerks pose like aloof runway models. Instead of communicating, "We are so glad you are shopping in our store," they patronizingly broadcast, "You should be grateful we allow you to enter our store." Consequently, I no longer spend any of my money in that clothing chain.

In a similar way, every youth ministry event has its own manner or attitude. There is an atmosphere or a feeling that stays with people after experiencing the program and interacting with the community. Setting the right tone is related to, but different from, developing a hospitable environment, which we focused on in chapter 2. The tone reveals how we view ourselves in relation to those who attend our gatherings. Tone is subtle, but it has significant implications. We want to set an accepting and welcoming tone, and avoid communicating an arrogant, exclusive, negative, or overly serious tone.

For instance, like the snobbish clothing store, we can transmit an attitude of spiritual arrogance. Because we are living for the Lord, we may peer steeply down our noses at those whom we deem to be less spiritual. We may be kind and benevolent to the "ignorant barbarians," but the glare of spiritual arrogance we send their way blinds them to accepting our community and message.

Sometimes we communicate that our ministry is a "members-only" club. Using "in language," treating outsiders with reserve, and referring to "in experiences" tells everyone that only the involved share our exclusivity. That great camping experience attended by only six of the program's thirty-five members becomes a divisive wedge when mentioned by those elite at every gathering!

There is also the negative attitude through which we subtly broadcast that our hearts are really not in what we are doing. As leaders we may lack enthusiasm and excitement about our work, and without knowing it exclaim, "This is hardly worth my time, let alone yours." Sadly, some young people may be genuinely open to the Gospel but end up disinterested because of the negative tone exuded by those who are supposedly proclaiming it.

Often we as leaders are oblivious to the tone of our own ministries. We become accustomed to the way we do things, and we do not recognize an arrogant, exclusive, or negative tone. Getting consistent and objective feedback from others is one way to keep us honest about what tone we are broadcasting.

Having become aware of some of the pitfalls of negativity, we want to develop a tone that communicates that we are thrilled to be serving others and are equally excited about everyone who walks in the door. We want teens to experience God's presence in what we are doing. Young people need to sense in us a difference that stimulates curiosity and interest in what we believe, and that causes them to consider the optimistic possibilities of their involvement in our ministry. We should operate as servant-leaders, focused entirely on those we are seeking to love into the Reign.

Additionally, our sessions should be fun. A tone of joy leaves people wanting to come back. Though we desire with all our hearts for teens to accept our sometimes urgent message to accept Jesus Christ's love for them, an overly serious tone will turn them away instead of drawing them back to hear more.

Setting an accepting, inclusive, joyful, and fun tone is evangelistic in and of itself because it draws people into our community, where they can experience the Gospel lived out.

## Establishing Teams Within the Large-Group Setting

Even with the best tone and our greatest intentions, it is still easy for individuals to get lost in a sea of teens, to be overwhelmed by the numbers and fall through the cracks. Experiencing a sense of belonging is a very important need of any adolescent. One practical way to impart a sense of personal belonging to participants is to use team competition in the large-group setting. Establishing small groups or teams that remain the same from one gathering to another helps the participants feel better connected with the large group. Making the young people members of teams builds in ways of developing community, friendship, and ownership. Those three elements are essential to holding the interest and participation of teens in outreach programming. Friendly competition among teens helps motivate them to come back. Additionally, it promotes outreach to their friends. Team competition is easily incorporated into the welcome and warm-up phases of the large-group evangelistic format.

## Using Team Competition

It is important to strike a balance when using team competition. We do not want an atmosphere of cutthroat, win-at-all-costs competitiveness. On the other hand, we do not want teens to be apathetic and bored with every competitive incentive. Competition should be fun, good-natured, and motivating. It should help draw people together, not tear them apart. Competition can be used in the following three areas.

### Attendance

Points can be awarded to teams for the participation of their members. A point system motivates teens to attend meetings because their participation will directly help their teams. It also prompts team members to encourage one another to come because the whole team will benefit if they do. Adult and teen leaders spearhead this effort initially, but as time goes on, whole teams become committed to it.

Additionally, points can be awarded to teams for bringing visitors—and those visitors can in turn be given an opportunity to become members of the teams. The incentive to invite friends inspires members to take part in the outreach process, and may even strengthen their own attendance as good friends become part of their teams. It is critical that the leaders of the teams emphasize people as opposed to points. We sincerely invite teens to our gatherings because we want them to be active parts of our teams—not because they are points that might help us win a competition. There is nothing more demeaning than feeling used in the name of "Christian love." Our plea is, "We have a great team, but it can only get better if you join us."

Teens are rarely evangelized as a result of attending a single gathering. To properly understand and respond to the Gospel, and be incorporated into the community, teens need to attend regularly. To ensure that we do not promote a revolving door of attendance, we can employ a point structure that rewards teams for following up on newcomers who continue to attend. By their fourth visit, participants should be considered not visitors but team members, and should be encouraged to invite their own friends to be a part of the team. Resource 3, "Team Attendance Sheet," and resource 4, "First-Timer Sign-in Sheet," can help you keep track of participation.

Because the teams are encouraged to grow by reaching out to others, they can become large—moving out of a small-group dynamic. I have seen teams grow from ten members to over forty. On the one hand, watching the numbers grow is exciting, but on the other, it can lead to some organizational challenges. The most effective way of addressing the latter is by adding adult or youth leaders. Those additional leaders should take responsibility for relating to a portion of the group and helping facilitate discussion time.

A recommended point structure for team competition is as follows:

| Participants | Points for Each Meeting Attended |
|---|---|
| First-time visitor | 1,000 |
| Second-time visitor | 2,000 |
| Third-time visitor | 3,000 |
| Team members<br>(A visitor becomes a team member at the fourth meeting she or he attends.) | 500 |

### Games

When using team competition, it is wise to choose a mix of games that rely on intellectual skills, athletic skills, other skills, and complete luck. Do not overuse games that favor any particular skills. Make the games fun to participate in and fun to watch. Some games might involve entire teams; others might call forth representatives of a certain class, gender, and so on. Encourage teams to cheer on their members, to boost morale and investment. Award points for the top three places. Enthusiastically announce the team scores and standings at the beginning of each meeting, and award a first-place trophy. You could also offer other incentives, such as first place in line at the refreshment table for the team that gets the most points at a meeting; a pizza party for the team that accumulates the most points during a month; an ice cream party for the three teams that earn the most points in six months; or, if your budget is like that of most parishes, an all-expenses-paid trip to Disney World for the team that stockpiles the most points in a year (okay, I am joking).

### Special Events

Special events or activities that earn team points can be used to motivate teens to apply the content of a session. For example, you might give teams 250 points for each teen member who memorizes a scriptural passage pertaining to last week's message. Other points might be awarded for service and for attendance at other events.

When team competition is done well, it motivates personal involvement, increases attendance and outreach, builds a sense of ownership and community, helps leaders focus their ministry on a particular group of teens, and provides fun in an electrically charged atmosphere.

(This section on team competition was adapted from Frank Mercadante, *Growing Teen Disciples,* pp. 170–172.)

## Developing an Evangelistic Outreach Spirituality

Growing up in an Italian family, I acquired some cultural values, beliefs, and practices common to my Italian heritage. From my earliest years, I believed that the kitchen was the center of life. I watched my grandmother and mother express their love to others by feeding them large quantities of food. I have met few Italians who do not share the belief that food is the nucleus of any worthwhile gathering.

Likewise, growing up Catholic, we learn to cherish certain values, beliefs, and practices. We embrace a common spirituality, or a shared manner of living and expressing our faith. For example, we value and participate in the Eucharist as a means of God's grace. Experiencing Jesus's presence in the Eucharistic celebration is central to our identity and spirituality as Catholics. Participation in the Eucharist defines who we are as Catholics.

Another essential element of being Catholic is being an evangelizer. Jesus calls us to share the Good News with all creation (Mark 16:15) and to make disciples of all nations (Matthew 28:18). In the apostolic exhortation *On Evangelization in the Modern World (Evangelii Nuntiandi),* Pope Paul VI calls evangelization the "'essential mission of the church'[1]" (sec. 14, p. 8). Pope John Paul II has spoken tirelessly about the need for a "new evangelization" (*Novo Millennio Ineunte of His Holiness Pope John Paul II to the Bishops, Clergy, and Lay Faithful at the Close of the Great Jubilee of the Year 2000,* sec. 40, p. 52).

> Over the years, I have often repeated the summons to the new evangelization. I do so again now. . . . We must revive in ourselves the burning conviction of Paul, who cried out: "Woe to me if I do not preach the Gospel." (1 Cor. 9:16) This passion will not fail to stir in the Church a new sense of mission. . . . Those who have come into genuine contact with Christ cannot keep him for themselves; they must proclaim him. A new apostolic outreach is needed, which will be lived as the everyday commitment of Christian communities and groups. (Sec. 40, p. 52)

Evangelization is as Catholic as the Eucharist, yet it has not been integrated into our Catholic spirituality in the same way. Catholics do not yet commonly share both the value and the practice of evangelization as an essential expression of their faith. Yet if we hope to change our world, we must become, as an entire Church, an evangelizing people. Additionally, if we hope to develop a parish youth ministry that has a comprehensive evangelistic approach (instead of an isolated evangelistic program), we need to build into it a culture of evangelization. We must integrate into our Catholic spirituality the call to share the good news of Jesus Christ with those around us. The following steps can help us develop an evangelistic spirituality in the leaders of our ministry:

**Model, live, and illustrate an evangelistic spirituality.** As leaders we must set the standard for those around us. If we are not evangelizing, we cannot expect others to do so. We should make a point to share our progress in evangelization (both the victories and the struggles) with one another. By the example of our own lives, we illustrate what it means to intentionally and spontaneously share our faith.

**Help foster in teens a personal, meaningful, and real relationship with Jesus Christ.** The apostle Paul revealed his motivation for proclaiming the Gospel when he spoke of being compelled by the love of Christ (2 Corinthians 5:14). He also stated that all things previously important to him were but rubbish in the light of knowing Jesus (Philippians 3:7–8). Being in a meaningful, personal relationship with Jesus Christ is a natural motivation for evangelizing. The richness of that experience compels us to want others to have it for themselves.

As leaders we must help foster in teens a personal and intimate relationship with Jesus Christ. If we give teens the vocabulary, the tools, and the communal support to truly know and love Christ, they will naturally want to share their experience with others—and that is evangelization.

**Teach and reinforce the understanding that people deeply matter to God.** The Lord was always looking out for the lost. Jesus invested his entire life for the sole benefit of others. His words, actions, and lifestyle demonstrated his deep love and care for all people. His final act of love on earth—dying in our behalf—was indicative of his entire life.

Jesus Christ loves everyone. He is truly in love with those we can hardly tolerate, let alone like. The people around us— whom we may love and cherish, find difficult or annoying, or not even know exist—are passionately loved by Jesus Christ. Their eternal destiny is everything to him—and it needs to become a priority to us. We must learn to value a soul beyond anything else. People will evangelize when they realize that the Lord loves people and has entrusted us with the task of populating his eternal Reign.

**Design outreach programming that intentionally attempts to reach the unevangelized.** Once our team members have caught the importance of inviting others to hear about and experience God's personal love, we must provide programmatic support for their efforts. Teens need an evangelistic venue to which they can bring their friends in order to share their faith. We should offer programming that articulates the Gospel clearly and relevantly and that teens can use as a springboard for further conversations of faith with their friends. Large-group evangelistic gatherings, as described in this book, are concrete examples of events that assist in evangelizing. Any youth ministry that wants teens to both value and practice evangelization must offer programming that intentionally proclaims the Gospel. Finally, we should continually encourage teens to invite their friends to the program's events.

**Provide teens with the training, tools, resources, skills, and accountability to share their faith with others.** Personally modeling evangelization, nurturing a heart for the eternal destinies of others, and providing evangelistic programming support is not enough to fully instill an evangelistic spirituality in teens. To become evangelizers, teens need training on how to share their faith interpersonally. Both adult and teen leaders should be equipped to share their faith journeys in a way that concretely illustrates the Good News. Leaders should be able to invite others into a new or deeper relationship with Christ. Evangelizers should be able to comfortably pray with those they are seeking to evangelize. In other words, we need to form skilled evangelizers who are capable of sharing their faith at any time, and we need to hold one another accountable to Jesus's call to proclaim the Gospel to all creation. For additional evangelistic resources and skill development, consult my book *Growing Teen Disciples: Strategies for Really Effective Youth Ministry* (Winona, MN: Saint Mary's Press, 2002).

## Conclusion

To "grow" your youth ministry and thus bring as many teens as possible into an encounter with the risen Christ, pay

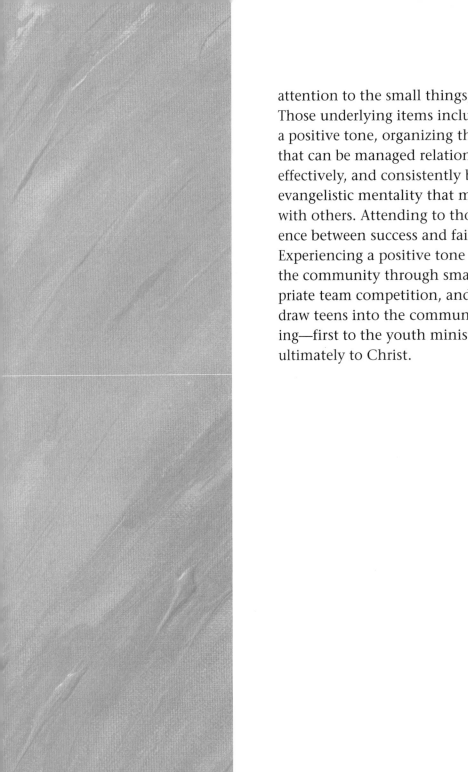

attention to the small things, the nuances and the intangibles. Those underlying items include establishing and maintaining a positive tone, organizing the large group into smaller groups that can be managed relationally, using team competition effectively, and consistently building in leaders and teens an evangelistic mentality that motivates them to share their faith with others. Attending to those areas often makes the difference between success and failure in programmatic endeavors. Experiencing a positive tone in the gatherings, feeling part of the community through small groups, participating in appropriate team competition, and sharing their personal faith each draw teens into the community; they enjoy a sense of belonging—first to the youth ministry and parish community, and ultimately to Christ.

# Team Attendance Sheet

**Team Name:** _____

**Team Number:** _____

**Team Leader:** _____

| Name | First-Timer x 1,000 | Second-Timer x 2,000 | Third-Timer x 3,000 | Team Member x 500 |
|---|---|---|---|---|
| 1. | | | | |
| 2. | | | | |
| 3. | | | | |
| 4. | | | | |
| 5. | | | | |
| 6. | | | | |
| 7. | | | | |
| 8. | | | | |
| 9. | | | | |
| 10. | | | | |
| 11. | | | | |
| 12. | | | | |
| 13. | | | | |
| 14. | | | | |
| 15. | | | | |
| Totals | | | | |

**Resource 3:** Permission to reproduce is granted. © 2004 by Cultivation Ministries.

# First-Timer Sign-in Sheet

| Name | Street | City, State, and Zip Code | Phone | E-mail |
|------|--------|---------------------------|-------|--------|
| 1. | | | | |
| 2. | | | | |
| 3. | | | | |
| 4. | | | | |
| 5. | | | | |
| 6. | | | | |
| 7. | | | | |
| 8. | | | | |
| 9. | | | | |
| 10. | | | | |
| 11. | | | | |
| 12. | | | | |
| 13. | | | | |
| 14. | | | | |
| 15. | | | | |

**Resource 4:** Permission to reproduce is granted. © 2004 by Cultivation Ministries.

# Getting Started

## The Nuts and Bolts
## of Evangelistic Outreach

Alex was the kind of guy who made moving a mountain seem
effortless. He had a compelling vision and motivated people
toward the fulfillment of his dream. He was a true leader who
knew how to rally the troops. Nevertheless, his youth ministry
team was falling apart at the seams.

Alex could sell, but he could not manage. He could motivate, but he could not administer. He could verbalize, but he
could not organize. The details of developing his ministry had
been sorely ignored, and as a result the program was about to
fail.

Fruitful youth ministries not only have a compelling
vision, a contagious spirituality, and roots in prayer, but are
also well organized. Youth ministries flourish when they are
relational, teen friendly, centered on discipleship, and well
managed. This chapter examines the details of organization
and some nuts-and-bolts issues that can keep the evangelistic
outreach machinery well oiled and running smoothly. It
focuses on organizing an outreach leadership team that is
effective, it discusses the role of teen leaders in outreach, it
explores the idea of building a culture of respect, and it looks
at ways to promote outreach events and to evaluate evangelistic impact.

### Organizing an Outreach Leadership Team

Working alone at a game of solitaire can be exhilarating;
working alone in youth ministry can be exhausting. Working
alone at solitaire is entirely appropriate; working alone in
youth ministry is not. Jesus (who, by the way, could have done
it alone) chose to work in community. If we are too busy to

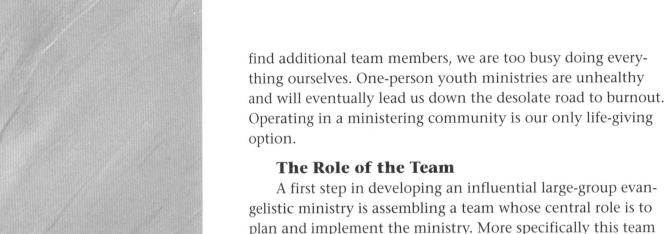

find additional team members, we are too busy doing everything ourselves. One-person youth ministries are unhealthy and will eventually lead us down the desolate road to burnout. Operating in a ministering community is our only life-giving option.

### The Role of the Team

A first step in developing an influential large-group evangelistic ministry is assembling a team whose central role is to plan and implement the ministry. More specifically this team is responsible for building and maintaining a base of intercessory prayer, constructing an evangelistically appealing environment, choosing session topics, developing meeting content and process, implementing programming, maintaining a relational approach, and evaluating the ministry. The team should gather as frequently as needed to effectively accomplish those tasks.

### The Team as a Community of Ministers

Too often the members of a ministry team have only their task in common. That is never enough, nor is it the model of the New Testament Church. Not only did the early Church have a commission to reach the world with the Gospel message (its task), but also its members were expected to love one another as a concrete example of the embodied Gospel. Furthermore, a community of ministers who passionately share a purpose and who love being with one another will be tenaciously resistant to the typical forms of ministry-threatening attrition. Ministry teams whose members share both mission and community are more likely to keep those members over the long term.

A portion of time should be reserved for building genuine Christian community within each gathering of the leadership team. That time might include sharing faith, reflecting on the Scriptures, praying with and for one another, and just plain having fun together. A community that has learned how to "rejoice with those who rejoice, weep with those who weep" (Romans 12:15) is well on its way to true fruitfulness.

### The Team's Need for Positive Group Processes

Having strong bonds with one another is an important outcome of taking time to build relationships among team members as well as building the youth ministry. Along with having a sense of belonging, team members also must feel that their purpose is being accomplished effectively and efficiently. Group processes—such as problem solving, decision making, conflict management, and communication between members—must be accomplished in a manner that motivates the team to continue to work together. If team members consistently leave meetings frustrated, exasperated, or in despair of ever accomplishing stated goals, then the team is ailing. When disgruntled team members gather outside official meetings to criticize those meetings' processes and decisions, the group is in need of urgent care.

## Decision Making by the Team

The team's decision-making process should allow the team to arrive at a quality decision quickly, the team members to be fully invested in and supportive of the decision, and the members to like one another afterward. Resource 5, "Seeking Consensus," and resource 6, "Communal Discernment," provide guidelines for two decision-making processes that can be effective in groups. Those resources can be distributed to the team members for their reference.

The key to leading an influential and smoothly running team is to maintain a balance between mission tasks and ministry relationships over time. Sometimes a meeting might lean to one side, but over the course of a year, the meetings need to generally maintain a balance between the two focuses. The following chart provides an example of a balanced format for a meeting of an outreach leadership team. Resource 7, "Meeting Facilitation," identifies the task and relationship functions associated with good meeting facilitation; that resource can also be given to the team members for their reference.

## Format for a Meeting of an Outreach Leadership Team

| Meeting Item | Purpose |
| --- | --- |
| Opening prayer (5 minutes) | Begin the meeting with a brief prayer that invites God's presence and direction. |
| Faither and life sharing (15 minutes) | Give the team members a chance to share what is going on in their lives and what God is doing in their lives. You might ask: "How is everyone doing? How is God working in your lives?" Lead the team members in ministering to one another through attentive listening, encouragement, and prayer for one another's needs. |

| Ministry training (15 minutes) | Lead a training session or discussion that helps to further equip team members in their role. This might include teaching new skills, discussing an article on evangelization, or presenting new research on today's adolescent. |
|---|---|
| Evaluation of previous meeting (10 minutes) | Evaluate every aspect of the previous evangelistic gathering. Use resource 8, "Evaluating an Evangelistic Gathering," as a tool. |
| Session planning (60 minutes) | Work through the details of the next evangelistic session. This might include determining topics, establishing objectives, developing an agenda, deciding on activities, contacting speakers, identifying resources, building a promotional plan, and securing prayer support. |
| Closing prayer (15 minutes) | Close the meeting by praying for all the needs of the evangelistic outreach and the entire youth ministry. |

## Recruiting Leaders

Recruiting a youth ministry team requires both spiritual and practical steps. Begin with a sincere and ongoing prayer that the Lord of the harvest will indeed send forth workers. Do not simply utter the Lord's Prayer unintelligibly and move on, but surrender your heart and the needs of the youth ministry to the Lord Jesus. If you begin your recruiting efforts by trusting the one who called the ministry into being, then you are laying a firm foundation on which to build.

Next determine practical steps you can take to recruit adults to the team. The best way of finding leaders who have the calling and charisms to work with teens is to ask key people to recommend individuals. Ask your pastor, parish staff members, past youth workers or catechists, parish council members, and teens. Once you gather names, either call the candidates or write them a personal letter, highlighting that they were recommended as persons gifted with an ability to work with teens. Resource 9, "A Selective Recruiting Letter," is an example. Be certain that you follow parish and diocesan policies regarding new volunteers (providing training, completing mandatory background checks, collecting required recommendations, and so forth).

Remember that recruiting ministry coworkers is an all-year-long task. As you develop relationships with fellow parishioners, you should look for people who might have a calling with teens. As soon as I started to research the purchase of a minivan, I noticed that every other vehicle on the road was a minivan! In the same way, when you start looking for potential youth workers, you will probably spot plenty all around you.

Once you have some potential leaders, it is time to provide them with information to help them discern their involvement. This can be done one-on-one or in a group. Usually the number of possible leaders will best determine your approach: a small number might warrant individual meetings, while a large number are best addressed all together. However, if you already have an established team that exudes enthusiasm and energy, consider a group setting even if the number of recruits is small. There is nothing better than exposing a potential leader to an attractive ministry community; everyone wants to be a part of a winning team.

Whether you meet one-on-one or with a group, you must cover several important issues. First, provide an overview of the entire youth ministry. Each potential leader should have an understanding of the big picture and how the evangelization ministry fits into the whole.

Second, help potential workers understand the specific vision, programming, and methodology of the evangelization ministry.

Third, describe the role of the outreach leadership team, including the responsibilities, time commitment, training, and meeting times. Any specific roles that need to be filled should also be explained.

You can expedite the process of disseminating that information by developing succinct descriptions that highlight the details of each ministry position. An outreach leadership team is more effective and efficient when each member takes on specific roles that capitalize on that member's strengths. The following descriptions are some possibilities.

**Outreach coordinator.** This person organizes the evangelistic outreach ministry. He or she oversees and facilitates the planning, implementation, and evaluation of the ministry and sessions.

**Games director.** This person researches, develops, chooses, and leads the games for each session. If established teams compete with one another, he or she keeps the team scores.

**Drama director.** This individual finds or writes suitable scripts, and directs the dramas or skits used in gatherings.

**Intercessory prayer director.** This director organizes a base of intercessory prayer to support the evangelistic outreach efforts.

**Promotions director.** This leader organizes all the publicity efforts for the program, including the production of announcements, fliers, and mailings.

**Small-group or team facilitator.** This person works directly with teens by leading a small group or team. Each facilitator is responsible for building relationships with teens, facilitating discussions, organizing small-group games and activities, motivating attendance and teen outreach, and sharing her or his faith.

**Hospitality director.** This director organizes and develops an attractive environment that makes teens feel accepted and cared for. Her or his responsibilities include welcoming the young people, writing and sending follow-up notes, and providing refreshments.

**Production director.** This individual is in charge of all the audiovisual needs of the program. His or her responsibilities include the preparation, setup, and running of all equipment, such as sound, video, lighting, computer, and projection units.

## Training and Supporting Leaders

I have heard plenty of horror stories about youth workers over the years. The most chilling but frequent tale describes how the victim—I mean, youth minister—is recruited in the fall, is given a program manual and a kind pat on the back, and is told: "It will all work out. See you in May." With that kind of preparation and support, no wonder the attrition rate of youth ministry exceeds that of a winter war in Siberia.

Youth leaders must not be abandoned, ill equipped and unsupported. The year should begin with preservice training that confidently launches them in their roles. First, leaders should have a clear understanding of the overall vision and programming of the youth ministry, in addition to an understanding of the purpose and goals of the evangelistic outreach program. Finally, the training content should focus on the skills and understanding necessary for leaders to accomplish their ministry.

Preservice training should be followed up with ongoing support and skill development that builds on the basics. Subsequent training needs can be addressed during the regular meetings of the leadership team.

Leaders should possess a good understanding of the dynamics and format of large-group evangelistic outreach. Because most sessions include small-group discussion, they also need good skills for leading discussions. Additionally, skills that help them initiate and build relationships with teens are essential. Furthermore, they should have good evangelization skills, such as the ability to share their faith journey and to share their faith interpersonally.

Finally, take time to support your leaders by affirming their gifts, encouraging them in their skills, and building authentic relationships with them. Always remember that a little gratitude goes a long way. Look for opportunities to say "Thanks."

## Incorporating Teen Leaders

As a young, ambitious youth leader, I did it all. I planned the meetings, opened with prayer, led the games, gave the talks, facilitated the discussions, closed with prayer, gave the ending announcements, and cleaned up afterward. In the end I was exhausted, the teens were bored with me, and our attendance declined. I had made our evangelistic outreach meetings spectator events, and the production was getting stale. The audience was tired and looking for a new show.

Finally, out of desperation and exhaustion, I opened the door for youth involvement in the planning and implementation of our meetings. As a result there was an immediate surge of fresh energy. Our gatherings became much more creative, more teens attended, and the teen leaders became highly invested in reaching out to their peers.

I have learned over the years that involving teen leaders is essential to effective youth ministry. I have also learned that before a young person is placed in a leadership role, he or she should understand and commit to the requirements of being a leader.

Those requirements include having a personal and committed faith life, a willingness to share one's faith, and a lifestyle that reflects the values of the Gospel. Ideally, young leaders should be formed into ministry teams that meet regularly to share an evangelistic vision, prayer, community, faith formation, and ministry training. Additionally, adult leaders should be committed to helping to spiritually form youth leaders, develop ministry skills among them, and supervise them. For more information on developing teen leaders and a powerful peer ministry team, see my book *Growing Teen Disciples: Strategies for Really Effective Youth Ministry* (Winona, MN: Saint Mary's Press, 2002).

Once teen leaders are trained and developed, they are ready to get involved in the planning and implementation of the evangelistic outreach programming. They can help choose the topics, develop the objectives, and create the talks, skits, games, and mixers. They can also lead the various activities, facilitate discussions, and develop a warm and inviting environment. By acquiring basic skills in interpersonal evangelization, teen leaders can follow up relationally with teen participants.

Even when teens have been prepared to assist with the evangelistic ministry, the key principle for teen ministry is to place them only in roles for which they have been adequately prepared and supervised. Never place them in unsupervised situations or in circumstances beyond their personal and faith maturity.

## Developing a Culture of Respect

I was once a guest speaker for a teen audience that, to put it kindly, were not very attentive. They sat in comfortable huddles, some even with their backs to me. They whispered, giggled, and generally paid little attention to what was going on up front. Their reception of my message was colder than an Alaskan snowdrift. The adult leaders stood passively against the walls, looking like they were working off a sentence of community service. I plowed through with as much passion as I could muster, but I knew my words were falling on deaf ears. Before I had ever arrived, the culture of this group had reduced the chances of anyone's getting anything out of any session.

The dignity of the Gospel we proclaim is such that we should carefully build a culture that creates the most favorable conditions for reflective consideration of the message. As leaders we have the power to build an environment of respect and receptivity. When I stood before three hundred teens at my parish's gatherings, the audience quickly became quiet and attentive. That response was not natural, but with careful engineering, it evolved into reality.

The creation of a culture of respect for one another is the task of the leadership. First, if the leaders want all eyes, ears, and minds to be focused on the speaker, they must model attentiveness and respectfulness themselves. Too often leaders set the worst example when it comes to listening. We can somehow feel that we have more important things to tend to, or we can easily lose interest because we are familiar with the program being presented. Not only can we become a distraction to the participants around us, but also our actions can say that listening to the speaker is not important. So the first step is for both adult and teen leaders to model a wholehearted attentiveness.

Second, leaders must gently reinforce respect for others by encouraging the attentiveness of the audience. Both adult and teen leaders should be placed throughout the crowd in case there are pockets of side conversations. Leaders cannot be clumped together in a corner or lining the perimeter of the room. Ministry team members can work in twos, and even be assigned sections by a room grid. If you are monitoring the audience and some people are talking around you, gently and kindly give a look that says, "Please don't talk." If they do not respond, say softly, "I am sorry, but I am having a hard time hearing our speaker." Because we want to maintain a positive, loving, and inviting environment, it is best not to function like a prison guard. If a teen does not respond to the gentle encouragement of a leader, then the message of that encouragement should be amplified. That can be accomplished by the nonverbal and verbal reinforcement of several additional leaders nearby. Eventually it becomes real apparent that it is entirely uncool to talk while someone is speaking up front.

Finally, be vigilant in example and in reinforcement. Over time your gatherings will develop the kind of social norms that enhance the teens' reception of your message. After a while being disrespectful of others will become a cultural taboo.

## Marketing an Evangelistic Outreach Program

A great evangelistic program, with prayerful and skillful leaders who are well organized, are models of respectfulness, and are partnering perfectly with well-equipped teen leaders, is utterly worthless if people do not know about it. In the end there is not much difference between an unattended but great outreach event, and a well-attended but horrific one; both are a waste of time. To put a lot of prayer, preparation, and effort into planning an evangelistic outreach and then not publicize it is nothing less than a sin.

Jesus spread the word of his "outreach gatherings" by sending his apostles ahead to announce to the inhabitants of a town that he would be arriving shortly. Likewise, if we are going to reach out to teens, then we better put time, effort, and creativity toward promoting our events. The following sections introduce some simple marketing approaches.

### Offer a Great Gathering

The best youth ministry marketing is to consistently offer a quality program. In other words, our gatherings speak for themselves. If teens find our programs to be worth their time, they will not only come back but will come back with their friends. So the first principle for marketing our program is to commit to excellence in our meetings. If we get that down, the rest of our marketing will be much easier.

### Choose a Good Name for the Gathering

A good name is not necessarily going to dramatically increase our attendance, but a bad name is a serious liability. Teens will refuse to go to an event that has a hokey or negative name.

Inviting teens to help name an outreach ministry program is always a good idea. Because our outreach is for teens, it is in our best interest to find a name that is attractive to youth. Most adults do not realize how dated their perspectives really are. We sometimes gravitate toward terms and language that were hip when we were young but are prehistoric today.

Also, a name should somehow communicate the purpose and personality of a program. It cannot just sound cool—it has to be meaningful and to describe the event it represents. Resource 10, "Naming Your Ministry," can help your team choose a good name for outreach meetings.

### Encourage Teen-to-Teen Promotion

The best publicity is always word of mouth. Fliers promote little interest if they stand on their own; fliers passed from one teen to another with a personal invitation have far greater credibility and impact.

Relying on teens to invite their friends is the best strategy for promoting events. To do that effectively, we must encourage both teen leaders and youth attendees to bring their friends.

First, teen leaders should know that the only reason we have an evangelistic outreach gathering is to reach out to the teens of our communities. It is reasonable to expect that they will always be praying about whom to invite and will actually be bringing their peers to the gatherings. As leaders we must reinforce the importance of our teens' reaching out, until it is a part of their Catholic spirituality.

Be careful not to let your teen leadership devolve into a youth group. The flip side of a cohesive group is that it can become an exclusive group that turns inward. Instead of inviting other teens to join, the group may actually unconsciously turn others away because they might threaten the comfort and security of what presently exists. Teen leaders need to understand that evangelistic outreach gatherings are not primarily for enhancing their own spiritual growth but for reaching the unevangelized.

Along with being encouraged to bring people who may not go to church or who have not been exposed to faith in Christ, teen participants should know that their friends are always welcome and wanted. Encourage everyone to come to the next gathering with a friend. Provide fliers, business cards, and other promotional tools that teens can effectively use to pass information to their friends.

## Employ Practical Promotion Ideas

The best type of promotional flier, brochure, or postcard in some way gets the recipient to do something. In other words, it is interactive. For instance, send a message in reverse type; to read it, a teen will have to hold it up to a mirror. Or send a teaser postcard that has only, in large type, a date (with no return address). Teens will study the postcard, call friends to see if they know what it means, and simply keep mulling the mystery over. Mission accomplished! Getting an active response to a communication is a great way to get teens talking about the event. Better yet, build a reputation for interesting, interactive, and creative publicity. Teens will look forward to and carefully study your mailings, instead of passively dismissing the predictably boring.

Other ideas: Send a flier or postcard referring teens to a personal ad in a local paper that tells what the next event is. Communicate an event through crossword puzzle clues. Make promotional T-shirts in the style of concert tour shirts; place your outreach program's name and logo on the front, and the meeting dates and topic titles on the back.

## Evaluating Evangelistic Impact

Finally, we can never pursue excellence without a commitment to ongoing evaluation. As hard as the truth may be, it is ultimately our friend. A ministry team should make a mutual agreement to be sensitively honest with one other while pursuing excellence. When protecting our own feelings becomes more important than giving one another honest feedback, our programs will suffer.

Also, we need to beware of getting entangled in a dead-end blame game. It is easy to blame everything around us for teens' lack of interest in our events. Whiningly criticizing parents, schools, or sporting events for negative results that are rightly deserved is the MO of the truly ineffective leader. When we fix our vision on everything but our own territorial waters, we anchor our ministry in the status quo. If teens are not returning to our events, then what we are offering is probably not worth their time. They will be polite and say, "I am so busy," but what they mean is, "I am too busy with the things I'd rather do."

We would do well to focus all our energy on truly loving our teens and building an absolutely excellent evangelistic outreach ministry. If we pour ourselves into those two endeavors, we will not have the time or energy to be sidetracked by unproductive, dead-end thinking.

Consider using resource 8 for evaluating your evangelistic outreach gatherings. Ask each team member to fill it out immediately after a gathering. Tally the combined results and share them during the following meeting of your leadership team. Evaluating with the goal of improving can be a positive team experience for everyone and will greatly benefit those who attend your program sessions.

## Conclusion

The best youth ministries are a combination of visionary leadership and detail management. Both perspectives and the skills associated with them are necessary to be truly fruitful in outreach ministry. Likewise, the effective organization of an outreach leadership team includes recruiting adult leaders and placing them in roles that capitalize on their strengths, incorporating teen leaders in outreach, building a culture of respect, promoting outreach events, and evaluating evangelistic impact.

Jesus, who could do it all, did not. He knew the value of gathering a community, caring about them as individuals, teaching them to care for one another, and then equipping them to share the Good News. Two-thousand-plus years later, we are striving to also be disciples of Jesus Christ and to bring the Good News to the teens of our parishes and schools. Let us take the time to form caring relationships, to extend our care to the teens entrusted to us, and to do all that we can to build an evangelistic outreach of which Jesus would be proud.

# Seeking Consensus

Consensus is reached when all members believe that the decision made is the best option under the circumstances and constraints.

## Contributing to Consensus Is Not . . .

- Giving in just to get it over with
- Holding on just to get your way
- Finding the least painful solution or simply compromising

## Contributing to Consensus Is . . .

- Being confident about the quality of the decision
- Believing that your input was allowed and valued
- Feeling that you can actively support the decision

## Steps to Consensus

1. Outline the decision to be made.
2. Define the process for making the decision.
3. Encourage diverse viewpoints.
4. Facilitate the process and reach a decision.
5. Test the conclusion.

(This resource is adapted from Cultivation Ministries, *Training for Strategic Youth Ministry Training Workbook* [Saint Charles, IL: Cultivation Ministries, 1991], page 15. Copyright © 1991–2003 by Cultivation Ministries. All rights reserved. Used with permission.)

 **Resource 5:** Permission to reproduce is granted. © 2004 by Cultivation Ministries.

# Communal Discernment

Communal discernment is a prayerful decision-making process in which we primarily seek to hear the Holy Spirit in one another. It is a process of surrendering our will to God by listening to what the Spirit is saying. Because there is one Spirit speaking to all those involved, the decision that is made must be unanimous.

> ## *The Practice of Communal Discernment*
>
> 1. State the decision to be made.
> 2. Prayerfully seek the guidance of the Holy Spirit.
> 3. Prayerfully surrender your personal agendas.
> 4. Discuss the different perspectives.
> 5. Listen to the Holy Spirit.
> 6. Discern direction.
> 7. Reach a unanimous decision.
> 8. Offer a prayer of thanksgiving.

(This resource is adapted from Cultivation Ministries, *Training for Strategic Youth Ministry Training Workbook* [Saint Charles, IL: Cultivation Ministries, 1991], page 13. Copyright © 1991–2003 by Cultivation Ministries. All rights reserved. Used with permission.)

# Meeting Facilitation

A meeting facilitator must balance the functions required to accomplish the group's tasks with the functions required to build a sense of community in the group.

## Task Functions

- Set the agenda.
- Monitor the time.
- Give instructions.
- Summarize the discussion.
- Clarify the issues.
- Facilitate discussion.

## Relationship Functions

- Encourage dialogue.
- Affirm team members.
- Resolve conflict.
- Allow all to share.
- Facilitate faith growth.
- Deepen the sense of community.

(This resource is adapted from Cultivation Ministries, *Training for Strategic Youth Ministry Training Workbook* [Saint Charles, IL: Cultivation Ministries, 1991], page 46. Copyright © 1991–2003 by Cultivation Ministries. All rights reserved. Used with permission.)

 **Resource 7:** Permission to reproduce is granted. © 2004 by Cultivation Ministries.

# Evaluating an Evangelistic Gathering

Please fill out the following evaluation. Rate each section and element on the following system: **5** = excellent, **4** = very good, **3** = good, **2** = average, and **1** = poor. Explain each assessment in the "Comments" section. If your rating is less than **5,** or excellent, state specifically what changes would improve it to excellent.

| | | | | | | |
|---|---|---|---|---|---|---|
| **A.** Hospitality | **5** | **4** | **3** | **2** | **1** |
| **1.** Greeting | **5** | **4** | **3** | **2** | **1** |
| **2.** Friendliness | **5** | **4** | **3** | **2** | **1** |
| **3.** Positive environment | **5** | **4** | **3** | **2** | **1** |

Comments:


| | | | | | | |
|---|---|---|---|---|---|---|
| **B.** Welcome and warm-up | **5** | **4** | **3** | **2** | **1** |
| **1.** Opening prayer | **5** | **4** | **3** | **2** | **1** |
| **2.** Mixer | **5** | **4** | **3** | **2** | **1** |
| **3.** Games | **5** | **4** | **3** | **2** | **1** |

Comments:


| | | | | | | |
|---|---|---|---|---|---|---|
| **C.** Message | **5** | **4** | **3** | **2** | **1** |
| **1.** Drama | **5** | **4** | **3** | **2** | **1** |
| **2.** Talk | **5** | **4** | **3** | **2** | **1** |
| **3.** Teen witness | **5** | **4** | **3** | **2** | **1** |
| **4.** Discussion | **5** | **4** | **3** | **2** | **1** |
| **5.** Evangelization | **5** | **4** | **3** | **2** | **1** |
| **6.** Interactivity | **5** | **4** | **3** | **2** | **1** |
| **7.** Topical relevance | **5** | **4** | **3** | **2** | **1** |
| **8.** Clarity | **5** | **4** | **3** | **2** | **1** |

Comments:

**D.** Closure                                              **5  4  3  2  1**
    **1.** Invitationalism                          **5  4  3  2  1**
    **2.** Persuasiveness of the message            **5  4  3  2  1**
Comments:




**E.** Follow-up                                           **5  4  3  2  1**
Comments:




**F.** Miscellaneous
    **1.** Transitions                              **5  4  3  2  1**
    **2.** Organization and preparation             **5  4  3  2  1**
    **3.** Preparation in prayer                    **5  4  3  2  1**
    **4.** Activity sequencing                      **5  4  3  2  1**
    **5.** Relationality                            **5  4  3  2  1**
    **6.** Other: _____         **5  4  3  2  1**
Comments:

# A Selective Recruiting Letter

After potential youth workers are identified, use the content of this letter to correspond with them.

Dear *(name)*:

As you may be aware, we are committed to the youth of our parish and to the development of a vibrant and relevant youth ministry. With that ministry as our goal, we recognize the importance of building a solid foundation of leadership that is capable of supporting and sustaining future growth and development.

Things have not changed much since Jesus said, "The harvest is plentiful, but the laborers are few" (Luke 10:2.) It is a rare moment in parish life when we have more workers than we can use, especially in our work with adolescents!

Even so we can never ignore the importance of selectivity. Programs are built on people. Our choice of people when building a foundation for youth ministry is absolutely critical to the future success of the ministry.

With all that in mind, I invite you to consider being a part of the adult leadership that will spearhead our new youth ministry. You were not randomly chosen out of desperation! Your receiving this letter is no accident; it is the outcome of a conscious and deliberate choice.

I was asked to recommend some people from the parish whom I feel have a contagious faith, can relate to young people, and will be effective youth workers. You are one of those people!

I am asking you to prayerfully and thoughtfully consider joining us in an information night for prospective adult leaders of our youth ministry program. The meeting will be held *(day)*, *(date)*, at *(time)*, at *(place)*. In that meeting you will receive a more clear and detailed description of what we are planning to do with the ministry. These are some of the issues we will address:

- What are the ministry's plan and strategy?
- What is the time commitment for youth workers?
- How might you benefit by being involved?
- What elements will help youth workers to be successful?
- How can you discern if this is your calling?

I hope to see you on *(day)*, *(date)*. If you are interested but are unable to attend the meeting, please call me at *(phone number)*. I will arrange to give you the information that will be presented at the meeting.

A multitude of voices are beckoning the allegiance of our young people. At no other time in the history of this country has there been such a diversity and quantity of voices. Unfortunately, the voice of the Church, which holds the greatest news of all—the Gospel of Jesus Christ—is sometimes reduced to a whisper among the deafening screams of the contemporary American youth culture. We need now, more than ever before, to be a significant voice in the lives of our young people. Please consider joining us in the effort do that.

In Christ's service,

*(Name)*
*(Title)*
*(Parish)*

(This resource is adapted from Cultivation Ministries, *Training for Strategic Youth Ministry Training Workbook* [Saint Charles, IL: Cultivation Ministries, 1991], page 47. Copyright © 1991–2003 by Cultivation Ministries. All rights reserved. Used with permission.)

# Naming Your Ministry

Your program's name should be thoughtfully and carefully chosen. It will become the herald of your message and ministry, it will express your program's identity, and it will create an important image.

## Describe the Program's Target Audience

- Who are they?



- What are their needs?



- What are their interests?



- What are they attracted to?



- What are their likes and dislikes?



- What motivates them?



## Describe the Program

- What are your program's mission, goals, and objectives?



- What is your message to the target audience?

- What are the benefits of involvement in the program?

- What is attractive about the program?

- What words describe your program?

## Describe the Program Elements
## Most Attractive to the Target Audience

- From what you have to offer, what will young people find most attractive?

- What will most interest them?

- What will most influence their environment?

## Brainstorm Possible Names

Jot down your ideas here:

## Evaluate Each Possible Name

- Is it appealing to young people?

- Is it true to your mission?

- Is it motivating?

- Is it easy to say and easy to remember?

- Does it communicate your program's personality?

- Is it distinctive?

- Will the teens be proud of it?

## Evaluate and Test-Market Each Finalist Name

Ask yourself and test-market subjects these questions:

- What does this name communicate to you?

- What kind of impressions does it leave you with?

- What do you like and dislike about it?

- Is it easy to say and easy to remember?

- Does it communicate your program's personality?

- Would you be proud to invite a friend to a program with it?

- Will youth be proud of it?

## Select and Market the Best Name

- Choose the best name.

- Design a logo to go with it.

- Write a descriptive statement about it.

- Publicize it!

(This resource is adapted from Cultivation Ministries, *Cultivation Strategy Workbook: Tools for Really Effective Parish Youth Ministry* [Saint Charles, IL: Cultivation Ministries, 2001], pages 6.10–6.14. Copyright © 2001 by Cultivation Ministries. Used with permission.)

# Part B

## Evangelistic Outreach Sessions

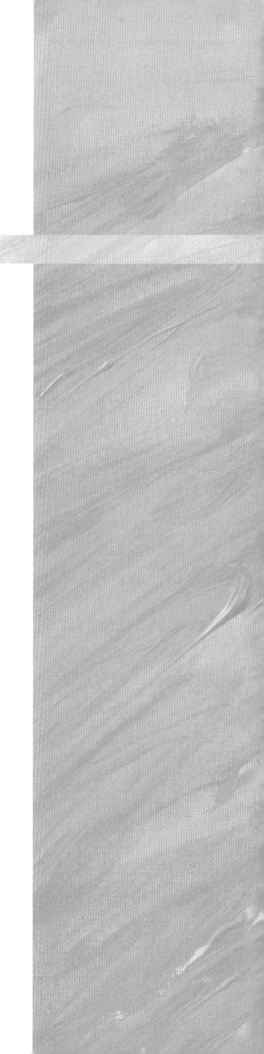

# Introduction

Chapters 5–10 provide six detailed sessions for evangelistic outreach. The sessions each last 90–110 minutes, and their content is designed for high school–aged teens but can be adapted for junior high participants. Each gathering focuses on a common perennial issue of adolescence or faith, such as friendship, self-worth, sexuality, peer conformity, view of God, and foundation for living. The sessions follow the objectives, guidelines, and format of the large-group evangelistic model explained in chapters 1–4.

When using a session, consider the personality and the developmental and spiritual maturity of your group. All activities may not work optimally in your particular setting. Feel free to make appropriate adaptations to fit your situation.

Here are brief explanations of the sections of the sessions:

**"Overview."** The overview introduces the session topic. Consult it to identify the focus of the gathering.

**"Theme" or "Themes."** The theme or themes succinctly capture the specific content of the gathering.

**"Schedule."** The schedule outlines the movements of the meeting, each activity within those movements, and the time allotted for each activity.

**"Objectives."** The objectives state what we hope the participants will come to value (affective), know (cognitive), or do (behavioral). They answer the question, "What are we trying to specifically accomplish by the gathering?"

**"Scripture Passage."** For each gathering, one Scripture passage is chosen to provide the scriptural basis for the message.

**"Related Scripture Passages."** In addition to the main scriptural text, several other biblical passages are provided to promote a broader scriptural understanding of the topic. These passages can be used as follow-up resources or to stimulate additional ideas.

**"Music Resources."** The music resource listings provide the names of contemporary songs that relate to the session topic. These songs can be played before or after the gathering, or both, to reinforce the message. They also can be used for follow-up or to stimulate additional ideas regarding the topic.

**"Materials Needed and Preparation."** All the necessary materials and preparation steps are given for each session. The items are listed in the order in which they are mentioned in the activities.

**"Procedure."** This section details each activity in the session schedule. It includes explanations, transitional ideas, and comments to help you understand the activities and how they relate to the theme or themes and to the gathering's sequence.

**Handouts and resources.** Each gathering includes one or more reproducible handouts or resources. Those materials contain statements for a mixer as well as scripts and narrations for actors and presenters.

# Chapter Five

# What Kind of Pig Are You, Anyway!?

## Building a Foundation That Can Withstand the "Huffs" and "Puffs" of Teenage Life

### Overview

Like the houses of the title characters in "The Three Little Pigs," the lives of teens need to be based on stable and solid foundations—in their case foundations that can withstand the storms of adolescence. Often young people build their identities and lives on less-than-reliable sources, such as peer groups, looks, romantic relationships, achievements, and if possible wealth. Jesus Christ and his words of life are the true foundation and cornerstone for living. Only when we are truly rooted in him can we both withstand the torrents of this life, and stand confident in the next life.

### Objectives

- To identify and understand common faulty foundations on which we base our lives
- To value Jesus Christ and obedience to his word and will as the most reliable foundation for living
- To invite or reinvite Jesus Christ to be the foundation of our lives by living according to the principles of the ROCK

### Themes

- Faith in Christ
- Making Christ our foundation for living

### Schedule

- Pregathering Hospitality
  - Team Prayer
    (15 minutes before start)
  - Greeting
    (10 minutes before start)
- Welcome
  - Introduction and Opening Prayer
    (5 minutes)
  - Brick Mixer
    (10 minutes)
- Warm-Up
  - Sticky Stacker
    (10 minutes) *or* Stability
    (10 minutes)
- Message
  - "The Three Little Pigs" Melodrama
    (10 minutes)
  - Teen Witness Talk
    (5 minutes)
  - Theme Introduction and Discussion
    (10 minutes)
  - "One Bad Day" Skits
    (10 minutes)
  - Keynote Presentation: Built on the ROCK
    (15 minutes)
- Closure
  - Closing Prayer: A ROCK Gift (10 minutes)
- Postgathering Follow-Up
  - Refreshments
    (15 minutes)

## Related Scripture Passages

- Jeremiah 16:5–8
- Matthew 6:19–21
- 1 Timothy 6:17–19
- 1 Peter 2:6–7

## Scripture Passage

Everyone then who hears these words of mine and acts on them will be like the wise man who built his house on rock. The rain fell, the floods came, and the winds blew and buffeted the house. But it did not collapse; it had been set solidly on rock. And everyone who listens to these words of mine but does not act on them will be like a fool who built his house on sand. The rain fell, and the floods came, and the winds blew and buffeted the house. And it collapsed and was completely ruined. (Matthew 7:24–27)

## Music Resources

- "My One Thing," performed by Rich Mullins, from the CD *Never Picture Perfect*, Reunion Records, 1989.
- "Upon This Rock," performed by The Newsboys, from the CD *Not Ashamed*, Star Song, 1992.
- "You're My Rock," performed by Becca Jackson, from the CD *It'll Sneak Up On You*, Word Records, 1997.

## Materials Needed and Preparation

- ☐ Gather the following items:
    - ❏ Decorations for the gathering space (see the preparation step that follows this materials list)
    - ❏ Tables
    - ❏ Name tags decorated with a brick background, one for each participant (optional)
    - ❏ Copies of handout 1, "Brick Mixer," one for each participant
    - ❏ Pencil or pens, one for each participant
    - ❏ Supplies for the "Sticky Stacker" game or the "Stability" game:

    ### Sticky Stacker
    - ☐ Paper plates, four for each team of ten
    - ☐ Graham crackers, three halves for each participant
    - ☐ Frosting, about one-half cup for each team of ten
    - ☐ Plastic spoons or knives, one for each team of ten
    - ☐ Masking tape
    - ☐ A watch, clock, or timer that marks seconds
    - ☐ Baby wipes, one for each participant

### Stability
  - ☐ Rectangular "bricks" for constructing a tower
  - ☐ Poster board and markers (optional)
  - ☐ A pair of dice
- ❏ Seven copies of resource 11, "'The Three Little Pigs' Melodrama"
- ❏ Newsprint and markers
- ❏ Eleven copies of resource 12, "'One Bad Day' Skits"
- ❏ Props for the second skit on resource 12 (listed on the resource)
- ❏ A candle and matches
- ❏ A Bible
- ❏ A large rock (real or made out of papier-mâché)
- ❏ Smooth, pocket-sized rocks (shale works well), one for each participant
- ❏ Paint and a small paintbrush, a paint pen, or a permanent marker
- ❏ Reflective music (optional)
- ❏ Refreshments
- ☐ The meeting room should be decorated to reinforce the theme of building on a solid foundation. Here are some possibilities:
  - Paint a backdrop of a brick foundation.
  - Stack cinder blocks to represent a solid foundation.
  - Display posters or a backdrop of the three little pigs and their homes.
  - Post building blueprints.
  - Post pictures or drawings of excavating equipment digging foundations.
  - Arrange a tableau of three large appliance boxes decorated to look like the houses of the three little pigs.
  - Present an electronic slide show (for example, using PowerPoint) that includes pictures of building foundations, storm-damaged property, the Scripture passage for this session, excavating equipment, the three little pigs, tall buildings, large rocks or mountains, and so forth.
- ☐ Consider setting up a registration table that provides name tags decorated with a brick background.
- ☐ Decide whether to use the "Sticky Stacker" game or the "Stability" game, and set up the room as necessary.

"Sticky Stacker" setup: Along one wall of the meeting room, line up tabletop work areas, one area for each team of ten. In each work area, place four paper plates. On one plate place three graham cracker halves for each

team member. On another plate place one-half cup of frosting and a plastic spoon or knife. Leave the third and fourth plates empty. About 8–10 feet from the opposite wall, mark a starting line with masking tape.

**"Stability" setup:** Obtain enough *same-sized* rectangular "bricks" to construct a tower that is three bricks square and 4–7 feet tall. The length of each brick must be three times the width; for instance, if the brick is 3 feet long, it should be 1 foot wide. (For the bricks, you could use baseball card boxes, children's cardboard building blocks, or two-by-fours cut into 10½-inch blocks.) Start the tower by laying three bricks side by side to form a square. Stack three bricks on top of them, turned 90 degrees so that they criss-cross the first three bricks. Continue in this pattern, alternating the direction of the bricks in each row. When you are done, you may want to place a poster board "Do Not Disturb" sign on the structure so that it does not get knocked over.

☐ Choose seven expressive and extroverted volunteers to be part of "The Three Little Pigs" melodrama. Provide each with a copy of resource 11. Explain that the characters are to act out their roles as the narrator reads the story, and the narrator should pause and give time for them to complete their actions.

☐ Ask a teen leader or a teen participant to give a 5-minute witness talk illustrating how Jesus Christ can become one's foundation for living through the experience of a teenager. Offer the following questions for reflection and for incorporation into the sharing:

- What were the faulty foundation or foundations of your life (for example, looks, achievement, friends, wealth, or romantic relationships)? How were they inadequate or in what ways did they fail you?
- Why did you begin to question those foundations?
- How did Jesus Christ and his word become your foundation?
- How has your view of yourself changed as a result?
- How has your view of others changed?
- How has your relationship with Christ and his Church changed?

Review the talk before the meeting. Provide constructive feedback to help ensure an excellent presentation.

☐ Consider noting the questions from step 1 of the activity "Theme Introduction and Discussion" on newsprint.

☐ Choose eleven teen leaders or participants to be part of the "One Bad Day" skits. Provide each with a copy of resource 12.

☐ You will want to become very familiar with the presentation portion of this session in order to share the message rather than read it.

☐ On a sheet of newsprint, write "ROCK."

☐ On the large rock, paint or mark, "Jesus, the ROCK." On each pocket-sized rock, paint or mark, "Jesus, my ROCK." Place the large rock on or near a table in the center of the room, and place all the participants' rocks on the table.

# Procedure

## Team Prayer (15 minutes before start)

Gather the ministry team together in order to get yourselves centered in prayer before the meeting. Begin by reading and reflecting on 1 Thessalonians 1:5. Pray for each activity and for those involved—both the ministers and the participants. Ask the Holy Spirit to bring to life each element of the gathering and to draw the participants to Christ, making him their foundation for life.

## Greeting (10 minutes before start)

Position both adult and teen leaders by the entrance doors and throughout the meeting room, to greet the participants as they arrive. Build an evangelistic climate from the moment teens arrive by creating a warm and friendly environment. Make sure that no one is standing alone.

## Introduction and Opening Prayer (5 minutes)

**1.** Enthusiastically welcome those gathered. Make special mention of newcomers. Briefly introduce the theme of the gathering, using the following example in your own words:

✦ Hello! My name is *(your name),* and I want to welcome you to *(your program's name).* Thank you for joining us this evening. I especially want to welcome any of you who are here for the first time. We are thrilled that you are with us.

✦ This evening's meeting is called "What Kind of Pig Are You, Anyway!?" We are going to look at how we can build the kind of foundation that can withstand the huffs and puffs of teenage life.

**2.** Offer a simple prayer that both invites God's presence and ties in the theme of the meeting. The following words offer an example:

✦ Lord, we invite you to be present in all we do this evening. May your Holy Spirit speak to our hearts and help us identify the things that fail to anchor us during the storms of life. May you be our rock and foundation. Amen.

## Brick Mixer (10 minutes)

**1.** Distribute handout 1, and pencils or pens. Then provide the following instructions in your own words:

✦ The goal of this mixer is to find different people who match the descriptions listed on the sheet.

✦ As soon as you find someone who fits a description, ask the person to sign your sheet.

✦ The first person to get all the brick descriptions on the sheet signed by others wins the game.

✦ When you are signing sheets, you may sign only descriptions that apply to you.

✦ Each of you may sign only one description on a sheet.

✦ You cannot sign your own sheet.

✦ Sign the bricks legibly using your first and last names.

✦ Once all the bricks in the foundation on your sheet are signed, come up front with the sheet.

**2.** After the winner is declared, invite her or him to come forward and read each description, and ask those who have signed each description to demonstrate it, explain it, or accept applause for it (for example, request that the person who is not afraid to sing in front of the group sing a song).

## Sticky Stacker (10 minutes)

Introduce the idea of a firm foundation with this game or the "Stability" game.

**1.** Divide the participants into teams of ten. Then point out the tabletop workstations and starting line for this activity, and provide the following instructions in your own words:

✦ The object of this game is to build a tower out of graham cracker halves and frosting. The team with the tallest and strongest tower wins.

- The cracker structure is to be built on one paper plate, cannot extend beyond the surface of the plate, and must be more than two cracker halves tall at the end of the game. Leave one paper plate at your workstation empty; it will be used during the judging of the structures.
- Each team will line up behind the starting line.
- On "Go" a player from each team will run to the team's workstation and begin building.
- Each team member will take a turn and has only 30 seconds to place three graham cracker halves on the team's structure. You may not add any more than three cracker halves during your turn.
- I will sound an alarm after 30 seconds, and the builder will stop, and a new team member will run to the table and continue with the building.
- If a person does not use three cracker halves in the allotted time, those cracker halves can no longer be played.
- If the structure begins to fall, a team member may use her or his turn to fix it.

Ask the participants if any of the instructions you have just given need to be clarified or repeated. Respond accordingly. If your teams are uneven, mention that some members of the smaller teams will have more than one turn.

**2.** Give the teams about 2 minutes to discuss their strategy for building.

**3.** Ask the participants to line up at the starting point and then allow the competition to begin. Remember to sound the alarm every 30 seconds until everyone has participated in the competition. Provide baby wipes so that the participants can clean themselves up after they are done building.

**4.** Regather everyone near the cracker structures, and determine a winner, using the following criteria:
- If a tower is fewer than two cracker halves tall—it is eliminated.
- Of the towers remaining, the one that bears the most weight wins.
- To determine which structure bears the most weight, place the unused paper plate over one of the towers. Then place on the plate objects used in this session, beginning with the lightest, such as an empty frosting can. Keep adding heavier objects, such as a box of graham crackers and a Bible, until

the tower collapses. Do the same for each tower, using the same objects in the same order, until you have a winner.

## Stability (10 minutes)

Introduce the idea of a firm foundation with this game or the "Sticky Stacker" game.

**1.** Ask for a volunteer to get the audience cheering for their teams and to offer verbal affirmation and amusing commentary during the game. Invite that person to come forward. Also invite volunteers to serve on three teams, with each team having no more than five players.

**2.** Refer to the tower you built before the gathering began. Then offer the following instructions in your own words:

✦ One person from the first team will run to the block structure. He or she has 20 seconds to remove one block from any layer except the top layer, without causing the structure to fall. If the structure remains intact, the runner should take the block back to the team. If the runner fails to complete the task within 20 seconds, the team will be disqualified from the game.

✦ The process will continue with one representative from each team completing the same task every 20 seconds.

✦ Team members may tap the blocks in the structure to determine which ones seem loose enough to remove.

✦ A team member may not use any body part to support the structure while pulling out a block or to keep the tower from toppling.

✦ Only one person is allowed at the block structure at any given time.

✦ Each team will be awarded 100 points for each block its members retrieve, and the team with the most points wins.

✦ The game is completed when the structure topples. The team causing the structure to topple automatically loses all its points and the game.

Ask if any of the instructions you have just given need to be clarified or repeated. Respond accordingly.

**3.** Designate one player from each team to roll a pair of dice. The team rolling the highest number gets the first turn, and so on. Lead the participants in playing the game until a winning team has been declared.

## "The Three Little Pigs" Melodrama (10 minutes)

Invite your seven actors to come forward and present the melodrama from resource 11. At the completion of the production, thank the volunteers for their assistance.

## Teen Witness Talk (5 minutes)

**1.** Introduce the teen leader or participant you have invited to share a witness talk. You might also introduce this portion of the gathering with these or similar words:

✦ Like the three little pigs, we can build our lives on shaky and unstable foundations. *(Teen's name)* is going to share with us the challenges of the "huffs and puffs" in building his (or her) foundation for living.

**2.** At the conclusion of the talk, thank the person who has shared and offer any comments you think might help the group move into the next portion of the gathering.

## Theme Introduction and Discussion (10 minutes)

Instruct the participants to gather into teams to discuss two or three of the following questions. You may wish to post these questions on newsprint.

✦ What is the moral of the story of the three little pigs? How is the story relevant to us, today?

✦ In what ways do you see the story of the three little pigs illustrated in teenage experience? How specifically do you see teens building lives like the first two pigs built their houses?

✦ What is a foundation? How do our lives have foundations?

✦ In most buildings, the foundation is somewhat hidden. Do you think that is also true in people's lives? How can we see, or know, what we have based our lives on?

✦ What is the foundation of your identity? What are some of its building blocks?

✦ On a scale from 1 to 10, where 1 equals "Fragile" and 10 equals "Invincible," how do you rate the foundation of your life and identity? Please explain your answer.

## "One Bad Day" Skits (10 minutes)

1. Offer the following comments in your own words:
   ✦ Society's values are often very different from those of the Gospel. The following skits illustrate the vulnerabilities of basing our self-worth, identities, or purposes for living on common, faulty foundations such as our money and possessions, or our looks and bodies. The worldly things we often value and even set as the foundation for our personal worth and importance could disappear at any moment.

2. Invite the eleven teen leaders or participants you have selected to present the skits on resource 12. Be sure to thank the actors at the completion of the skits.

## Keynote Presentation: Built on the ROCK (15 minutes)

1. Introduce the presentation in the following way:
   ✦ While astronauts are in space, they float about their spaceship. They are weightless and therefore need to strap themselves into place to ensure they do not drift away! Suction cups attached to their shoes secure them to the floor; when they want to be released, they simply twist their feet. To push a button, they must be tethered in place, or they will be propelled in the opposite direction. Like astronauts in space, we need to be fixed in place in order not to drift directionless in life. We need a foundation that roots us in truth. As Jesus wisely warned, we need to build our lives on the ROCK.

2. Post the newsprint on which you have written "ROCK." Then continue with comments like these:
   ✦ The following talk will examine how we can experience a solid and true foundation for living that can withstand the storms of life, if we learn to do these things:
      ◇ *R*ecognize faulty foundations
      ◇ *O*btain our true worth and dignity and purpose from God
      ◇ *C*are for others as fellow children of God
      ◇ *K*eep our relationship with Jesus Christ living and active

3. Proceed with the presentation as follows, using your own words:

- Like all structures, our lives are built on foundations. Our identities as people are rooted in something. Like the houses of the three little pigs, our foundations for living can be strong and can weather the storms of life, or they can be inferior in substance and can collapse under pressure. Among the common foundations that lack the ability to provide us with an earthquake-proof identity are looks and body, wealth and possessions, friends, romantic relationships, and achievements.

- Some people base their identities on *physical appearance*. They root their value as people in looks and body. They reason, "I am lovable because or if I am physically attractive." In a culture that highly values physical beauty, it is no wonder that people might gravitate toward this faulty foundation. What makes this foundation as weak as a house framed in balsa wood is its inability to last. Looks change over time. Skin breaks out in zits, hair falls out and grays, weight is easier to gain as the metabolism slows, and age spots, wrinkles, puckers, scars, sagging chests, and drooping muscles all diminish attractiveness over time. If the basis of who we are is determined by our looks, we are not going to feel very good about our lives as we grow older.

- Others base their identities on *possessions*. They root their value as people in what they own or how wealthy they are. This foundation also has serious vulnerabilities. Financial situations can change drastically. Stocks can plummet, people can lose jobs, economies can falter, and possessions can be stolen, lost, or destroyed. Again, ultimately each of us longs to be loved and considered valuable for who we are, not what we have. Basing our identities on what we have will ultimately fail us.

- Still others find their value as a result of the status of their *friends*—"Cool friends, cool me." If they hang out with people who are "somebody," or popular, somehow that makes them "somebody," or popular. You've heard of guilt by association; this is cool by association. This foundation is as reliable as ice on a lake in eighty-degree heat. Eventually you're going to sink if you build your life on it. Sometimes friendship costs more than we are willing to pay, or friends change, or people move. Besides, deep inside we want to believe we are valuable because of us, not because of those who surround us.

✦ And still others build their identities on their academic, athletic, or artistic *achievements*. Achievements are certainly worthwhile and mark exceptional efforts. However, they tend to lose their value over time. Trophies collect dust, and academic awards become a thing of the past. At some point we reach the pinnacle of success, and our abilities decline. Besides, we all, deep inside our hearts, want to be loved because of who we are, not what we have accomplished. Basing our identities on accomplishments can put us on a treadmill of ever-increasing speeds. Sooner or later we cannot keep up.

✦ A man was driving along a country road when he turned his head and noticed a chicken running alongside his car. His speedometer read 50 miles per hour. The chicken was overtaking him as he increased his speed to 60 and then 70 miles per hour. The chicken's speed exceeded 70 miles per hour and then it turned into the driveway of a small farmhouse and disappeared into the field near the farmer's house.

The man was so fascinated by the chicken's speed that he pulled over and knocked on the farmhouse door. When a farmer answered the door, the man burst with excitement, saying, "Do you know that you have a chicken that can sprint over 70 miles per hour?"

The chicken's owner rubbed his chin and replied: "Oh, you must have seen our three-legged chicken. He's pretty fast. Yeah, there's three of us here, my wife, my son, and me, and when it comes to eating chicken, we always fight over who gets the drumsticks. In an attempt to save our family, we decided to breed three-legged chickens."

"Wow," said the man. "I've never heard of three-legged chickens! How's the breeding going? How do they taste?"

The farmer replied: "I don't know. We haven't caught him yet!" (adapted from a story by Buddy Hackett).

✦ The farmer's pursuit of the three-legged chicken is symbolic of a person's attempt to build the foundation of her or his identity on fleeting elements such as looks, possessions, friends, or achievements.

✦ The only lasting foundation for our identities and purposes comes from God. God's love for us is unchanging and constant. It does not depend on our looks, wealth, social status, or achievements. Instead of striving to be somebody important, we can be at true peace because God has already declared our importance. The Apostle John said, "But to all who received him, who believed in his name, he gave power to become children of God" (John 1:12). The reality of our relationship with God gives us true dignity, significance, and purpose.

✦ Being loved for our looks, wealth, social status, or achievements will always leave us with a nagging question: "Does anyone love and value me for me?" The good news is "YES!" God loves us unconditionally. Additionally, God has a purpose for each of our lives. The prophet Jeremiah states, "For surely I know the plans I have for you, says the LORD, plans for your welfare not for harm, to give you a future of hope" (Jeremiah 29:11). We are somebody special because God declares us so. In the mind of the most powerful being in the universe, we are important and loved. The omnipotent (all-powerful), omniscient (all-knowing), and omnipresent (all-present) Creator declares that he loves us.

✦ As children of God, we should treat others as our brothers and sisters. We should recognize and respond to their true worth.

✦ A wealthy man lost his wife when their only child was young. A housekeeper was hired to take care of the girl, who lived only into her teens. Heartbroken from this second loss, the man died a short time later. No will could be found, and because there were no relatives, it looked as if the state would get his fortune. The man's personal belongings, including his mansion, were put up for sale. The old housekeeper had very little money, but there was one thing she wanted. It was a picture that had hung on a wall in the house—a photo of the girl she had loved and nurtured. When the man's property was sold, nobody else wanted the picture, so she bought it for just a few pennies. At home she began to clean it and polish the glass. As she took it apart, a paper fell out. It was the man's will, and in it he stated that all his wealth should go to the one who loved his daughter enough to buy that picture.

- The truth about who we are in God's eyes has to be reinforced each day by building a daily and living relationship with Jesus Christ (John 15:1–8). Our relationship with Christ is built by communicating continuously (giving thanks, asking, and listening), sharing experiences (participating in the liturgy, the sacraments, and service), and telling others about our relationship with Jesus Christ.
- What are the building materials of your life? What is your foundation constructed of? The popular culture surrounding us offers plenty of sand on which to build our lives. It says that we are what we have, we are what we look like. The problem with sand is that it cannot hold a life in place when the wind picks up. Jesus Christ, on the other hand, can firmly root our lives in the truth of his Gospel. We are who Jesus Christ says we are: beautiful in his eyes, worth so much to God that Jesus died for us, and created for a wonderful purpose. Jesus Christ invites you to allow him to be the ROCK of your life.

## Closing Prayer: A ROCK Gift (10 minutes)

**1.** Dim the lights and light a candle to signify the transition to prayer.

**2.** Proclaim Matthew 7:24–27. Allow a moment of silence. Then offer the following comments in your own words:
- We are so glad each of you chose to come tonight.
- I hope you had a chance to get to know some other people and to hear, perhaps for the first time, that Jesus Christ wants to be the foundation of your life.
- He is the ROCK that you can rely on; you can find security in him alone, both now and forever.
- Jesus Christ loves you more than anyone ever will.
- I invite you to come forward and choose one of the rocks on the prayer table. Take your rock home and think about what *ROCK* stands for and talk to God about it.
- Jesus Christ calls you to "recognize" the faulty foundations of this world. He invites you tonight to "obtain" or find your true worth and dignity and purpose from God. He asks that you "care" for those around you as fellow children of God. And he challenges you to "keep" your relationship with him living and active in

order to stand firm in the truth of God's love every day of your life. Be founded on the ROCK!

**3.** Invite the teens to come forward one by one, to take a small rock from the prayer table as a symbol of their willingness to invite Jesus Christ to be the ROCK and foundation of their lives. You may wish to play some reflective music during this time.

**4.** Conclude with comments such as these:

✦ If you have any questions about how to ask Jesus Christ to be the foundation of your life, feel free to talk with me or any of our team members. We will be happy to share with you how we have invited Jesus Christ to be the foundation of our lives.

✦ Please stick around for refreshments, and we hope to see you at our next gathering, on *(day, date)*, at *(time)*.

## Refreshments (15 minutes)

Young people will stick around after the meeting if there is something to eat. Use this postgathering follow-up time to further establish relationships with teens, find out what they thought of the session, and continue to share your faith one-on-one. Remember: the best large-group evangelization does not stand solely on its program but is undergirded by a web of relationships that reinforce the evangelistic message interpersonally.

# Brick Mixer

The goal of this mixer is to find different people who match the descriptions listed on this sheet. As soon as you find someone who fits a description, ask that person to sign his or her first and last names in its brick. The first person to get all the brick descriptions on the sheet signed by others wins the game.

As you participate in this mixer, keep in mind these rules: You may sign only descriptions that apply to you, you may sign only one description on a sheet, and you may not sign your own sheet. Write legibly, using your first and last names.

| I am not afraid to sing a song in front of this entire group. | I got at least two A's on my last report card. | I play at least two sports at my school. |
| --- | --- | --- |

| My best friend is here. | There is someone in this room I would like to date. | I am a good friend. I do not gossip. |
| --- | --- | --- |

| I would like to be rich someday. | I am an aunt or an uncle. | I actually like my siblings. |
| --- | --- | --- |

| I get along well with my parents. | I have memorized at least one Scripture passage. | My faith influences my morals and decisions. |
| --- | --- | --- |

| My faith is the most important dimension of my life. | I read the Bible today. | I can recite the Ten Commandments. |
| --- | --- | --- |

 **Handout 1:** Permission to reproduce is granted. © 2004 by Cultivation Ministries.

# "The Three Little Pigs" Melodrama

## Cast

- Narrator
- Mama Pig
- Realtor
- First Little Pig
- Second Little Pig
- Third Little Pig
- The Big Bad Wolf

## Story

Once upon a time in a land far, far away, there were three little pigs who began to grow hair on their chinny chin chins and therefore were declared of age. They were about to leave the comfort of their home and their mother's watchful eye to enter the big city. This was a sorrowful day for Mama Pig, who lamented the sight of her children, ready to venture from the security of her safe dwelling. She affectionately squeezed the snouts of her three little piggies (as was her particular custom). As they skipped away, she sobbed and wailed uncontrollably.

After traveling for some time, the three little pigs found three plots of land in a row that were for sale. They were so ecstatic about their fortunate find that they began to hop up and down, hugging one another. They immediately found the Realtor who was selling the land and squealed in a harmonic chorus: "We want it! We want it! We want it!"

"Well," said the woman, as she sinisterly smirked and then slicked back her greasy hair, "the land is yours for only the microscopic amount of . . . a couple million bucks!" The little pigs' eyes bulged out of their sockets, and their mouths gaped opened in astonishment. They hung their heads in unison and began to slowly and sadly trudge down the road in despair.

"Wait!" The saleswoman exclaimed. "I was just joking! HA! HA! HA! The land is yours for only five hundred dollars!" Relieved, the three little pigs again hopped up and down, hugging one another in celebration. The real estate saleswoman became exhilarated at the sight of the deliriously delighted piggies and joined them in their festivity. The three little pigs handed over their money, and each claimed a plot of land on which to build a house. The First Little Pig

**Resource 11:** Permission to reproduce is granted. © 2004 by Cultivation Ministries.

claimed the first plot of land, the Second claimed the second, and the Third claimed the third.

The First Little Pig preferred immediate gratification. He did not want to be bothered with the complexities of building a solid house. He gathered small pieces of straw and quickly built a large and flimsy (but very comfy) hut. Because he finished before his siblings, he took out a lawn chair, relaxed in the sun, sipped lemonade, and worked on a tan.

The Second Little Pig spent a slightly greater amount of time on her house, but she also did not think too much about its stability. She scraped together a pile of somewhat-sturdy sticks and began to build a somewhat-sturdy structure. When she finished, she got out her boom box and played her favorite disco CDs. She then invited some of the coolest pigs over and danced half of the night away.

The Third Little Pig was the worker in the family. He thought long and hard about his house. Afterward he bought cement mix at the town store, mixed it with water, and churned it until his muscles were sore and almost all his strength was gone. The sun beat down on his forehead, and he wiped the sweat from his brow and armpits. He began to build the house, laying one brick at a time. He worked all through the hot afternoon. The sun set, and he kept working. The stars came out, and he was still working. The first two pigs left their lawn chair and boom box, and crawled into bed, and he was *still* working. Finally, he finished, went inside, locked his door, and fell fast asleep. How wonderful it was for each little pig to sleep soundly in his or her own home. Their snoring could be heard throughout the land.

While the pigs dreamt, the Big Bad Wolf confidently sauntered up the road toward their houses. When he reached the First Little Pig's hut, he licked his lips and shamelessly salivated. He howled in a deep and deafening voice, "Little pig, little pig, let me in!"

Startled, the First Little Pig felt his bladder give out as he jumped out of bed. He peered through the peephole of his door and quaked in terror. When he saw that it was the wolf, he was frightened but determined to protect himself. He mustered all his strength and feebly uttered, "Not by the hair of my chinny chin chin."

The wolf was angered, and he threatened: "Fine! Then I'll huff, and I'll puff, and I'll blow your house in!" And that's exactly what he did. The house went crumbling to the ground while the little pig just stood there frozen in panic. Only when the wolf licked his lips and began to charge his delicious prey did the sniveling little pig begin to move. The wolf chased him all over his plot of land, in zigs and zags and squares and circles. Before long the little pig decided to seek shelter in his sister's house of sticks. He swung open the unlocked door of the Second Little Pig's house, slammed it, locked it, and joined his sister under the bedcovers, shivering uncontrollably.

The sound of all this chaos awakened the Second Little Pig just in time for her to hear the wolf say, "Little pigs, little pigs, let me in!" Figuring that this house made of somewhat-sturdy sticks could withstand the wolf's huffs and puffs, they leapt out of bed and replied with naive assurance, "Not by the hair of our chinny chin chins!"

The nefarious wolf now seethed with fury. "Fine! Then I'll huff, and I'll puff, and I'll blow your house in!" he savagely snarled. The two little pigs stood confidently in the house, with their arms defiantly folded, sure that the wolf wouldn't be able to blow it down.

Unfortunately, sticks are only sticks, and the house was much too flimsy to save the pigs. It too went crashing to the ground. The wolf chased the two little pigs around their property in zigs and zags and squares and circles. Before long they ran to the Third Little Pig's door. With the wolf close behind them, the two little pigs pounded desperately on the locked door. Just as the wolf was about to sink his long, sharp claws into their backs, the Third Little Pig scooped them through the door and locked it tightly behind them. There was a loud thud as the wolf's body crashed into the door.

By now the wolf was emotionally raging and ravenously hungry. "Little pigs, little pigs, let me in!" he thundered. The little pigs were completely confident that this house would withstand a tornado, let alone a weak and weary wolf. "Not by the hair of our chinny chin chins!" they gleefully squealed.

"Haven't you had enough?" the wolf roared. "Fine! Then I'll huff, and I'll puff, and I'll blow your house in!" The wolf took a huge gulp of air and blew at the brick house. It didn't budge. He tried again, this time sucking in so much air that he let out the loudest, most gross belch in the history of civilization. He thought his lungs were going to burst before he blew out a brutal gust of hot air. The house stood strong.

The three little pigs frolicked in their formidable fortress as the woeful wolf slumped away, licked and famished. He knew that the house the Third Little Pig had built would never crumble, no matter how many times, and how strongly, he huffed and puffed. The wolf walked off into the distance. And the three little pigs lived happily ever after in the house with the solid foundation.

(This resource is based on "The Three Little Pigs," in Joseph Jacobs, *English Fairy Tales* [New York: Alfred A. Knopf, 1890], pages 73–76.)

# "One Bad Day" Skits

## Skit 1: Money and Possessions

### Cast

- Rich (a stereotypical rich kid; Rich has based his identity, self-worth, and reason for living on his material wealth)
- Dad (Rich's dad; his business is playing the stock market)
- Lighting technician

### Script

**Rich:** *(to audience)* Well, what can I say. I'm definitely the coolest and, may I humbly add, the richest person in my school. My name, Rich, says it all. I mean, I am outfitted exclusively in Abercrombie and Fitch, and I drive a brand-new Corvette that the girls just go nuts over. I have everything a guy could want, and more. For example, last week I asked my dad for an inground pool with a diving board. So guess what he got me? An inground pool with a diving board AND a waterslide AND a high dive. Good thing my dad's such a great investor; when it comes to buying the right stocks—he's the man!

*(Dad walks in, looking very distraught.)*

**Dad:** Rich, I have some bad news. . . . Ah. . . . How do I say this?

**Rich:** What? What's wrong, Dad? Was your *Wall Street Journal* delivered late again?

**Dad:** Son, I am afraid it's much worse than that. We've been so well off because I've played the market so well. I had a hunch, like I did years ago with that little software company, Microsoft. I did the research, like I did years ago when I bought a thousand shares of that little hamburger joint, McDonald's. I trusted my instincts, Rich, and invested everything in what I thought was going to be the next multimillionaire-making enterprise. But the market is unpredictable, Son. Atari computers just took a terrible plunge. . . . Who would've ever thought? We're bankrupt.

**Rich:** What are you saying, Dad?

**Dad:** We're going to have to sell the house and your car. Now, I know this is a shock to you—it was to me too. We're just going to have to tough it out.

**Rich:** But . . . the pool! . . . My Corvette! . . . And the girls that go nuts over it! . . .

**Dad:** I know, Son. I didn't say it would be easy, but we can do it. I've been looking for a new place to live, and I think you'll like what I've found. In fact, it's sitting in the driveway as we speak—

**Rich:** What is sitting in the driveway?

**Dad:** *(excitedly)* Oh, you're going to love it, Richy. It's our new trailer, of course! Kind of exciting, isn't it, Son?!

**Rich:** *(moaning despairingly)* Nothing's left, and soon all my friends will be gone, just like all our money. . . . My life is over! What's that in my shoes?! *(leans down and takes a shoe off)* Sand. How'd that get in there?

*(The lights dim.)*

 **Resource 12:** Permission to reproduce is granted. © 2004 by Cultivation Ministries.

# Skit 2: Looks and Appearance

## Cast

- Jenny (a high school student who suffers from self-absorption; she bases her self-worth on the way she looks)
- Mom (Jenny's mom; she encourages Jenny's vanity)
- Jeff (a boy in Jenny's class; he is curious about and fascinated with dermatology)
- Teacher (Jenny and Jeff's biology teacher)
- Three gawkers (actors who are planted in the front row of the audience)
- Lighting technician

## Props

- Two chairs
- A handheld mirror
- A tube of skin concealer
- A backpack
- A chalkboard or a dry-erase board

## Script

*(Jenny is getting ready for school, putting on make-up in the mirror and engaging in positive—and somewhat conceited—self-talk.)*

**Jenny:** Wow, Jenny, you sure are looking HOT today! In fact, you are beyond hot; you sizzle, woman—you're the original Cover Girl.

*(All of a sudden, Jenny spots a small blemish on her nose.)*

**Jenny:** *(absolutely hysterical)* Mom! Mom! Mom!

**Mom:** *(running onstage)* What's wrong, honey? Are you all right?

**Jenny:** No, I am NOT all right. Just look at my nose!

**Mom:** Dear, it's just a little pimple. You will be fine. Here's some concealer *(hands Jenny the concealer).*

**Jenny:** Thanks, Mom. You're a lifesaver. You and Clearasil, that is *(holds up the concealer).*

*(Both laugh ditzily.)*

*(Jenny puts on her backpack and heads to school, walking in place, waving and posing for friends. At the same time, Mom walks backward in sliding motions, giving the illusion that Jenny has "walked" to school.)*

*(Jeff enters with two chairs; he and Jenny sit down in a classroom setup. At the same time, Teacher wheels a chalkboard or a dry-erase board onstage and begins silently writing, "Biology Lab," on the board.)*

**Jeff:** Hey, Jenny, did you know there's like a funky fungus dilating on your face?

**Jenny:** What?! What are you talking about?

**Teacher:** What seems to be the problem, Jeff?

**Jeff:** Well, there seems to be some type of dermatological malformation growing on Jenny's nose, sir. By its size, structure, and mucus excretion, I would tend to classify it as some type of fungal colony.

**Jenny:** Shut up, dork! It's a zit.

*(Teacher approaches Jenny, looking sympathetic.)*

**Teacher:** *(awed)* Actually, Jeff, it's viral, but I could see how you could have thought it was a fungal colony because of its boil-like appearance and puslike excretions. The ring around the carbuncle leads me to believe that it is a mutant form of ringworm, but a second look makes me think. . . . *(rubs his chin, thinking)* Wow! Amazing! Class, gather around! This could be something you will never again see in your life.

*(Jenny is mortified throughout her "examination.")*

*(Gawkers planted in the front row of the audience come up to gather around Jenny, saying: "Wow! Cool!")*

**Teacher:** Jenny seems to have a massive infestation of warts, with a bacterial inflammation. This disease can be incurable and infects the extremities, causing gross dermatological malformations. And it looks and smells bad, too! Students! Just look, don't touch—this is extremely contagious.

*(Jenny races out of the room, mortified. As she is running, she stops and reaches in discomfort to her shoe.)*

**Jenny:** What's in my shoe! How did sand get in here! *(limps off)*

*(The lights dim.)*

# Chapter Six

# Treating
# the Chameleon Syndrome

## Peeling Off
## the Grip of Peer Pressure

### Overview

A chameleon is a lizard that has the unique ability to change the color of its skin to match its surroundings. It does that as a measure of protection from potential threats. Likewise, in response to peer pressure, adolescents can be tempted to change from their true colors to conform with the people surrounding them. We call that the chameleon syndrome. In this session we examine why it is important for teens to belong, and offer some practical steps for resisting negative peer pressure and allowing Jesus to be the person of greatest influence in their lives.

### Objectives

- To examine why pressure peer is so powerful in teens' lives
- To identify positive peer pressure as a form of protection from social predators
- To offer some practical steps for resisting negative peer pressure and allowing Jesus to be the person of greatest influence

### Themes

- Peer pressure
- Conformity
- Being grounded in God's love
- Being free to be ourselves

### Schedule

- Pregathering Hospitality
  - Team Prayer
    (15 minutes before start)
  - Greeting
    (10 minutes before start)
- Welcome
  - Introduction and
    Opening Prayer
    (5 minutes)
  - Peer Factor Mixer
    (10 minutes)
- Warm-Up
  - Play-Doh Challenge
    (15 minutes)
- Message
  - "Carl Chameleon"
    Skit (10 minutes)
  - Teen Witness Talk
    (5 minutes)
  - Theme Introduction
    and Discussion
    (10 minutes)
  - Keynote Presentation:
    Peer Pressure
    (15 minutes)
- Closure
  - Closing Prayer:
    Invitation to Acceptance (10 minutes)
- Postgathering Follow-Up
  - Refreshments
    (15 minutes)

## Related Scripture Passages

- Romans 12:14–21
- Ephesians 4:17–19,22,28–29,31–32
- Ephesians 5:18
- 1 Peter 1:14

## Scripture Passage

Do not be conformed to this world, but be transformed by the renewing of your minds, so that you may discern what is the will of God—what is good and acceptable and perfect. (Romans 12:2)

## Music Resources

- "Diamond," performed by Jump 5, from the CD *Jump 5 All the Time in the World*, Sparrow/EMD Records, 2002.
- "I Don't Care What It Takes," performed by Plus One, from the CD *Plus One Obvious,* Atlantic Recording, 2002.
- "What if I Stumble," performed by DC Talk, from the CD *Jesus Freak*, Chordant Records, 1995.

## Materials Needed and Preparation

☐ Gather the following items:
- ❑ Decorations for the gathering space (see the preparation step that follows this materials list)
- ❑ Blank name tags in different shapes and colors, one for each participant
- ❑ Colored pens
- ❑ Three or five blindfolds
- ❑ A large basket or bowl filled with candy or gum, one or two pieces for each participant
- ❑ Modeling clay (for example, Play-Doh), 2 cups for each team of ten
- ❑ A table
- ❑ A watch, clock, or timer that marks seconds
- ❑ Six large index cards
- ❑ A bell
- ❑ Ten copies of resource 13, "'Carl Chameleon' Skit"
- ❑ Props for the skit on resource 13 (listed on the resource)
- ❑ Newsprint and a marker
- ❑ Masking tape
- ❑ Refreshments

☐ The gathering space should be decorated to reinforce the themes of how peer pressure influences us and how we can stand against it. Here are some possibilities:
- • Furnish the room in black and white. Minimize the presence of colors as much as possible.
- • Arrange for some members of the leadership team to be dressed as mimes (with white faces, black makeup, black

pants, and white shirts, or vice versa). Have them mingle, saying nothing, and greeting people by shaking their hands and mimicking their facial movements and body language.

- On the wall put black-and-white banners with common statements reflecting the effects of peer pressure, like these:
  - ○ If I don't do it, what will they think of me?
  - ○ Everyone is going. I'll be left out if I don't.
  - ○ He'll love me more if I . . .
  - ○ She'll think I'm boring if I don't  . . .
  - ○ Everyone does it; how can it be so bad for me?
  - ○ No one else pays attention to those people; why should I?
- Play repetitive music in the background, something that gives the impression of going on and on, over and over.
- Place a picture of a large chameleon on the wall, and underneath it pictures of teens all dressed exactly the same as one another, all doing the same thing. In contrast, put a picture of Jesus on the wall, and underneath it pictures of teens all dressed in different styles and doing different activities.

☐ Mark half of the name tags with a 1 and half with a 2, so that you can use them to break the group into teams for the activity "Peer Factor Mixer." Set out the tags and colored pens for the greeting period.

☐ Ask a team leader to brief the volunteers in the mixer.

☐ For the activity "Play-Doh Challenge," place 2 cups of modeling clay for each team on a table at the front of the meeting room. Also write each of the following terms on a separate index card: "chameleon," "twins," "mask," "volcano," "child of God," and "strength."

☐ Recruit ten teen leaders or participants to assist with the skit in resource 13. Provide each with a copy of the resource and ensure that the volunteers practice before the meeting.

☐ Recruit a teen leader or a teen participant to give a 5-minute witness talk focusing on the role that peer pressure plays in that person's life and how he or she is dealing with it. Ask the volunteer to reflect on the following questions:

- How has peer pressure made you change, or want to change, to fit in? Have you ever behaved like a chameleon? If so, describe the situation.
- How does your faith in Christ help you respond to peer pressure? Give examples.

- Have you ever felt positive peer pressure from friends? If so, how did it help you? How can Christian community help us be ourselves?

Meet with the teen a few days before the outreach, to review the content and time frame of the talk and to provide encouragement.

☐ Consider noting the questions from the activity "Theme Introduction and Discussion" on newsprint.

☐ You will want to become very familiar with the presentation portion of this session in order to share the message rather than read it.

# Procedure

## Team Prayer (15 minutes before start)

Gather the ministry team together in order to get yourselves centered in prayer before the meeting. Begin by reading and reflecting on Romans 15:7. Then pray for each activity and for those involved—both the ministers and the participants. Ask the Holy Spirit to bring to life each element of the gathering and to help the participants experience the freedom to be themselves and to know that they are loved and accepted by God. As a team thank God for the opportunity to serve. Pray for eyes to see others as Jesus does and hearts to accept others as Jesus does.

## Greeting (10 minutes before start)

Position your ministry team by the entrance doors and throughout the meeting room. Enthusiastically welcome each young person as she or he arrives. Make sure that no participant is standing alone. As you greet the young people, pray for them quietly. Point out the name tags and instruct everybody to personalize one.

## Introduction and Opening Prayer (5 minutes)

**1.** Welcome the group enthusiastically. Your level of excitement will help set the pace and attitude of the participants. Help make newcomers especially welcome by making special mention of them. Briefly introduce the theme of the gathering, saying something like this:

◆ Hello! My name is *(your name)*, and I want to welcome you to *(your program's name)*. Thank you for joining us this evening. I especially want to welcome any of you who are here for the first time. We are thrilled that you have joined us.

✦ This evening's meeting is "Treating the Chameleon Syndrome." We are going to look at how we can be free from the grip of peer pressure so that we can be ourselves.

**2.** Invite the participants to join you in prayer, beginning with the sign of the cross. Say a simple prayer that both invites God's presence and ties in the themes of the meeting. The following words offer an example:

✦ Lord, we invite you here this evening. Help us to experience how much you love and accept us, just as we are. Help us to be ourselves and not to be pressured into doing things that would harm others or ourselves. In Jesus's name we pray. Amen.

## Peer Factor Mixer (10 minutes)

**1.** Ask for three or five volunteers (depending on the size of your group). Tell them to leave the room with the designated team leader, who will explain to them their role in the game. When they are outside the meeting room, the team leader should blindfold them and explain that the rest of the group is being divided into two teams. When they return to the meeting room, both teams will give them directions, and they are free to choose which to follow. One set of directions will lead them to a prize; the other set will send them away from the prize.

**2.** Once the volunteers have left, instruct the rest of the participants to go to one side of the room if their name tags have a 1 on them, and to the opposite side if their tags have a 2. Place a basket or bowl of candy or gum halfway between the teams, and to one side of the room. Tell them that team 1's goal is to guide the volunteers to the container by using verbal instructions. Explain that if the majority of the volunteers go to the container, then team 1 will get the treats.

Next explain that team 2's job is to keep the volunteers away from the container by using the same method. If team 2 gets the majority of the volunteers to stay away from the container, then team 2 will get the treats. (Actually both teams will get treats, but do not reveal that until the end of the game.)

**3.** Bring the volunteers back, announce "Go," and give the teams 3 minutes to direct the volunteers. Once a volunteer reaches the treats, take that player to team 1 and tell him or her to sit down, take off the blindfold, and be quiet until the game is over. If a player walks away from the prize and toward the other side of the room, take that player to team 2.

**4.** At the conclusion of the game, announce the winning team. Then regather the participants and pass the treats around and invite all the participants to take one or two. Explain that this mixer is much like life. We hear many voices telling us which way to go, and we can choose which way to go.

Ask the volunteers why they chose to go to a particular side of the room—toward the prize or away from it. Ask them how it felt to have many voices talking to them all at once.

**5.** Conclude by pointing out that one team was trying to get the volunteers to do something, and the other was trying to get them not to do something. Just like the teams, we can influence others toward something or away from something. We can encourage people to do things that will bring positive consequences or things that will bring negative consequences.

## Play-Doh Challenge (15 minutes)

Divide the group into its established teams, or create teams of ten and assign each team a number. Then offer the following information in your own words:

✦ Many forces mold us into the people we are—a lot of them positive and some not so positive. We have the power to choose what and whom we allow to influence us.

✦ In this game you will mold clay.

✦ On "Go," one member from each team will proceed to the table and view a term written on a card that I will place there. That person will return to the team with a clump of clay, and will have 30 seconds to represent the term by sculpting the clay, without using letters or words. He or she may not speak or use gestures during this process.

✦ Once someone guesses the correct term, that person runs to the front of the room and rings this bell. All the teams must stop working when they hear the bell, and send up another player. I will show the new players another card, and they will return to their teams to mold the next term.

+ The teams will get one point for each term that they guess correctly.
+ The team with the most points at the end of the game wins.

Ask the participants if any of the instructions you have just given need to be clarified or repeated. Respond accordingly. Conduct the game and announce the winner.

## "Carl Chameleon" Skit (10 minutes)

**1.** Introduce this portion of the gathering with these or similar words:
+ Both of the games we have played illustrate how we can be influenced by and influence others. The skit that follows features Carl Chameleon, a guy who just does not know who he is.

**2.** Invite the actors to come forward and present the skit as outlined on resource 13. Be sure to thank them at the completion of the skit.

## Teen Witness Talk (5 minutes)

**1.** Introduce the teen leader or participant you have invited to share a witness talk, using these or similar words:
+ Carl Chameleon was not sure of himself and was therefore easily swayed by peer pressure. We have likely all felt that we needed to act a certain way to be accepted.
+ *(Teen's name)* is here to share with us an experience of peer pressure and what he (or she) has learned about self-acceptance.

**2.** At the conclusion of the talk, thank the person who has shared and offer any comments you think might help the group move into the next portion of the gathering.

## Theme Introduction and Discussion (10 minutes)

Instruct the participants to gather into teams to discuss two or three of the following questions. You may wish to post these questions on newsprint.
+ In what ways do you see peer pressure exhibiting itself? How do you see it expressed at your school?
+ How has peer pressure made you want to change to fit in? Have you ever behaved like a chameleon? Explain your answers.

- Have you ever felt positive peer pressure from friends? If so, how did it help you?
- What, if anything, does accepting yourself have to do with how you respond to peer pressure?
- Do you believe that God loves you, just as you are? What difference could that make when others ask you to do something that you know would not be good for you?

## Keynote Presentation: Peer Pressure (15 minutes)

Offer the following presentation in your own words:

- It seems as though since we were in elementary school, some adult has been telling us what to do. Adults tell us to "just say no," to resist doing drugs or drinking when our friends tell us to. They tell us to "do the right thing" and be our own people—or at least be the right people for them. As if all that would solve all our problems!
- "Don't have premarital sex." "Don't swear." "Don't get bad grades." "Don't, don't, don't . . . *donuts, donate, done it . . .* " We stopped listening after the millionth "Don't."
- Practically everyone wants to fit in and have friends. Sometimes you want to change who you are or your morals so you can just hang out and be cool. But you could easily take that to an extreme. Extremes often start with little, innocent things that aren't that big a deal. Soon you find that those little things have taken over your life. Say you go to basketball practice after school on Friday and join in the dirty jokes and bad language. Seems harmless. *You* know you don't really mean it. Then you go home, and have a nice dinner with your folks, and pretend that you don't swear up and down at school. Saturday evening you go to a party and get trashed on beer, even though you think it tastes like turpentine—which you figure doesn't matter because after a few drinks, you can't taste it anyway. Sunday morning you go to church and youth group and pretend like you actually *are* holier-than-thou. Everyone seems fooled!
- But you can't pull one over on God. That's the perk of being God: he knows everything about everyone, all the time. In Jeremiah 1:5 he says, "Before I formed you in the womb I knew you." That means God made you

with special talents and gifts. God loves you for who you really are, under all the personalities you create so that you can "fit in."

✦ You're more than a sister or a soccer player, more than a jock or a musician, more than a friend or a boyfriend. John 1:12 says, "To all who received, who believed in his name, he gave power to become children of God." That's who you really are: a child of God.

✦ Maybe you're thinking: "Oh, sure. I'll be who God made me to be, his child, and everything will be *fine!* But who am I really? What's this 'child of God' nonsense? How do I know who I am? And what if people still don't like me anyway?"

✦ God knew you'd have those questions. When you're a child of God, you belong to him. Think about your strengths and qualities. Are you really good at art? Can you hit home runs like nobody's business? Are you a great listener? Can you stand on your head and spit wooden nickels? Those are all gifts that God gives. If you take a long look at where your skills and gifts lie, you'll be able to see how God designed you.

✦ If you can see who God made you to be, who other people want you to be is no longer important. You can just be yourself. If they don't like it, they lose out. Yeah, that's easy to say, but it's also true. Most people earn respect by being real, rather than by trying to be everything to everyone.

✦ There are a few things you can do to make sense of your situation.

✦ First, know that you are special to God, and that you are *exactly* who he wants you to be. Right down to the eye color, inch, pound, freckle, and sense of humor. He knew what he was doing when he created you, and he created you special. He made you for a reason, with unique talents and skills, and he'll take care of you.

✦ Next spend some time in prayer. Ask God to tell you who *he* wants you to be. Try *listening* for a response or a prompt. It may not be a booming voice, parting the clouds, saying: "Jimmy, you are going to be a doctor. Why else do you think you really enjoyed ripping your sister's dolls apart when you were six?" No, it usually doesn't work like that. Maybe God will send a friend to help you understand yourself. Whatever path you think you are being led down, know that who you are doesn't depend on who others *think* you are. You are who you and God decide you are, no more, no less, and you're just perfect that way.

✦ Accept yourself. Then picture yourself at church, at home, at school, at band practice, at wherever you go and whatever you do. See yourself being authentic in each scene, not caring who thinks what about anything you say or do. Then be that self! If others don't like the authentic you, it's their problem. And really, they often want you to conform just because they don't feel comfortable with themselves.

✦ Finally, spread the love. Spread it like butter on toast. If you want to be yourself, encourage others to be themselves too.

✦ Everyone wants to feel loved and accepted just as they are. No one would change themselves if they thought they could have friends without doing so. It's sort of time-consuming and complicated to keep switching personalities. If you don't believe me, recall that time you accidentally swore in front of your parents because you forgot to turn the swearing switch to off. Yeah, you probably got in trouble. The next time you're around people who are behaving in ways that don't feel right to you, remember that there's no need to pretend to be like them. Be authentic, and other people will feel like they can be authentic too.

✦ Figure out who you are. Ask God for his input. Accept yourself for who God made you to be. Then accept others as they are.

✦ And remember this one last thing: There is no "cool" or "uncool" in the Reign of God. When Jesus walked the earth, he attracted every loser, sinner, prostitute, reject, and nerd around, because he loved everyone no matter what. Love yourself no matter what. Love others no matter what.

Move right into the closing prayer, as though the talk is actually continuing.

## Closing Prayer: Invitation to Acceptance (10 minutes)

**1.** Briefly share one example of why belonging to Christ has helped you to accept yourself and others better. Point out that, just like the volunteers in the activity "Peer Factor Mixer," we can choose what we are going to do as individuals, and that we can also choose what influence we are going to try to have on others.

**2.** Give the participants a moment of silence to think about what struck them from the session. Then make comments like these:

✦ Perhaps you are being pressured to do things you really don't want to do, and you would like to make some different choices. Perhaps you are pressuring others, and you know that you are leading them down a path that is harmful. Perhaps you are applying some positive peer pressure to help a friend make better choices. Perhaps you are dealing with self-acceptance and wondering if God really does love you. Right now is the time to invite God into all of those places.

**3.** Lead the participants in the following prayer:

✦ Lord Jesus, you created each of us and love us as we are. Help us to appreciate the gifts and qualities you have given us. Help us to encourage others in their strengths and to be strength for them in times of weakness. Help us to make decisions that will lead others and us closer to you. Help us to live as your children now, and to be ourselves. Protect us from all evil and from influences that would lead us away from you. Please forgive us for the times we have pressured others into doing wrong. Please help us to walk away from anything that would hurt others or us. We ask these things in your name.

**4.** Invite the participants to give one another a sign of acceptance. Demonstrate by shaking your neighbor's hand or hugging your neighbor; saying, "I accept you as you are"; and prompting the other person to respond, "And I accept you too."

## Refreshments (15 minutes)

Young people will stick around after the meeting if there is something to eat. Use this postgathering follow-up time to further establish relationships with teens, find out what they thought of the session, and continue to share your faith one-on-one. Remember: the best large-group evangelization does not stand solely on its program but is undergirded by a web of relationships that reinforce the evangelistic message interpersonally.

# "Carl Chameleon" Skit

## Cast

- Carl Chameleon
- Joe Jock
- Athletic Adam
- Cher Leader
- Chrissy
- Roland
- Al Coholic
- Anita Buzz
- Valerie Dictorian
- Brian Brains

## Props

- Athletic gear (for example, a sweatshirt, a basketball, a football, tennis balls, a tennis racquet, a *Sports Illustrated* magazine, and Gatorade or some other bottled sport drink)
- Religious gear (for example, a shirt with a religious saying, a big Bible, a bottle of holy water, a scapular, a cross, and a rosary)
- A watch
- Druggie gear (for example, a torn T-shirt, worn-out jeans with holes, cigarettes, beer cans, a pipe, a spike collar, and dog chains)
- Smart-kid gear (for example, a button-down shirt, a bow tie, glasses, a pocket protector, a calculator, and a stack of books)

## Script

**Carl:** Hi. I'm Carl Chameleon. I'm in high school, and I guess you could say I'm pretty average. I want to belong, just like everyone else. And, I'll admit, sometimes that makes me want to compromise on my morals. But I guess a lot of people go through that in high school. You can probably identify with me a bit. Oh, hey! Here come Joe Jock, Athletic Adam, and that hot chick, Cher Leader!

*(Carl begins putting on athletic gear, and Joe, Adam, and Cher begin making their way toward Carl.)*

**Carl:** Oh, man, these are the coolest kids in school. And Cher is so hot I get weak kneed and tongue-tied when she's around. But she only dates football players, or basketball players if they're lucky.

*(Joe, Adam, and Cher arrive.)*

**Joe:** Hey, Carl, whassup, my man?

**Carl:** Not much. I'm doin' fine.

**Adam:** 'Sup, Carl! *(gives a high-five secret handshake)*

**Cher:** Hey there. How's it goin'? Didn't I see you at the football game on Friday?

**Carl:** Yeah, I thought I'd check it out. That's where everyone is on a Friday night. So, what did you guys do this weekend?

**Joe:** Oh, man, it was sports nonstop. We played basketball, we played tennis with our folks at the club, there was the football game on Friday, and we practiced soccer with Adam's little brother and a whole other ton of stuff to raise money for a charity on Saturday.

**Adam:** Man, was that a workout! It was awesome!

**Carl:** Yeah, that sounds sweet!

**Joe:** Then on Saturday night we got our hands on some steroids to enhance our performance. Gotta keep an edge on the competition, you know? It's so cool. Not only do we play better, but our voices are getting deeper, we're getting more chest hair, the whole deal!

 **Resource 13:** Permission to reproduce is granted. © 2004 by Cultivation Ministries.

**Adam:** And I drank so many protein shakes I threw up more than I did when I got wasted the weekend before last!

**Carl:** Wow, that's so cool.

**Adam:** So, Carl, what did you do this weekend?

**Carl:** Um, I couldn't be at that sports-a-thon on Saturday because, um, I was running in that half marathon in the city. It was a great way to start off my active weekend. It only took up Saturday morning, so I was still able to fit in some basketball and a few laps of swimming at the Y. That evening I played football with some friends, then lifted and read *Sports Illustrated*. You know, I've got a subscription.

**Joe:** That's cool, man.

**Cher:** Wow, Carl, with all that I bet you could be an ironman triathlete!

**Adam:** Well, Carl, we gotta jet. We're going to try to pack in at least eight hours of football 'cuz it's Monday and all, and there's an indoor soccer game this evening. So what are you doing?

**Carl:** Oh, um. . . . I'll be watching those games too. Nothing like an eight-hour marathon stretch of football!

**Cher:** Cool. See ya.

**Adam:** Later, Carl.

**Joe:** Later, my man.

*(Joe, Adam, and Cher depart.)*

**Carl:** Wow, they're so cool. Oh, no, here come Chrissy and Roland. They are so holier-than-thou. I hear they pray over eight hours a day and actually *read* the bibles they got for Confirmation!

*(Chrissy and Roland arrive, and Carl changes into religious clothes.)*

**Chrissy:** Peace of Christ, Carl!

**Carl:** Uh, you too, Chrissy.

**Roland:** God is good? . . .

**Carl:** *(looks confused)*

**Roland:** Carl. . . . God is good?

**Carl:** Oh, yeah; sorry. All the time! And all the time . . .

**Roland:** God is good! There you go, brother!

**Chrissy:** Isn't it good to be here together, as a small faith community at our school, so we can love and serve the Lord?

**Carl and Roland:** *(together)* Amen!

**Chrissy:** Oh, I am so spiritually high from that all-night prayer vigil we had.

**Roland:** I said the rosary over four thousand times before passing out from exhaustion. It was so awesome!

**Carl:** Wow, sounds . . . really great. I was praying too, this weekend. I took part in that twenty-four-hour Bible-a-thon. I read the entire Bible; it was great. But since I've done that a few times this month, I went from Revelation to Genesis rather than front to back. Then, of course, I read *Catholic Digest* front to back. I've got my own subscription, you know.

**Chrissy:** Praise the Lord, Carl. Well, we're going to go now; we have to be at Mass at eight.

**Carl:** *(looks at his watch)* It's only five.

**Roland:** We like to spend a few hours in prayer to prepare for it.

**Chrissy:** Then, after that, Roland will be receiving that reward from Mother Teresa's order for being an outstanding Catholic youth. You're going to be there, aren't you?

**Carl:** Um, no; I've got the altar server meeting to lead, and then I have to go to that vocations talk for prospective priests.

**Roland:** Go with God, my brother. *(makes the sign of the cross)*

**Chrissy:** Lord bless you, friend. *(genuflects)*

**Carl:** God is good?

**Chrissy and Roland:** All the time!

**Carl:** I'll see you two later!

*(Chrissy and Roland leave.)*

**Carl:** Man, they are whacked out. I bet just being seen with them is enough to get you a "get into heaven free" card. Oh, man, here come Al Coholic and Anita Buzz. They are so cool. They have so many drugs in their blood.

*(Anita and Al head over, and Carl changes into druggie clothes.)*

**Anita:** Like, HIGH, Carl. Get it? High?!
**Carl:** For *sure,* man.
**Al:** How's it flowin', my man?
**Carl:** Just tryin' to fly HIGH to get through the day, you know.
**Anita:** You should have been with us this weekend, Carl. We did so many different drugs, we were seeing quadruple.
**Al:** Yeah, and we solved the global warming problem.
**Carl:** Oh, yeah? What's the answer?
**Al:** *(laughing)* I can't remember! I forgot sometime between puking in the sink and puking in the toilet.
**Carl:** Sounds tight. I partied all weekend too. I must have drank four cases of beer on Friday night, and I was still so hungover on Saturday that I couldn't get out of bed. It's a good thing I had *High Times* to read. I've got a subscription, you know.
**Anita:** Man, that's awesome. Well, we gotta split; we got some serious tokin' to do tonight. Al just got a new bong from this place online. It says you get a 40 percent better high and 20 percent less brain damage. It was bargain priced, too.
**Carl:** Cool; I'll have to check it out.
**Al:** Hey, Carl, you wanna come?

**Carl:** Aw, man, nah, not this time. I've already got to go to this other party where someone's older brother got, like, four kegs or something.
**Al:** Cool. Next time then, man. Next time.
**Anita:** Check ya later, man.

*(Al and Anita walk away.)*

**Carl:** Wow, those guys don't have a whole lot upstairs anymore, but they do seem to have a lot of fun. Oh, no, here come Valerie Dictorian and Brian Brains.

*(Carl begins changing into smart-kid clothes.)*

**Carl:** Those two are hands-down the smartest individuals in the school, maybe anywhere. They're always "most likely to gross $100 million by the age of thirty" in the yearbook. They sure seem like they've got it all together. Just talking with them makes me want to dig out my dictionary to figure out what they're saying.

*(Valerie and Brian make their way over.)*

**Valerie:** Greetings and salutations, Carl. Have you computed the answer to that mathematics problem yet?
**Carl:** Not as of yet; I'm still working on chaos theory.
**Brian:** Wonderful. I'll check in with you later for your results. I'm curious as to how they will affect the theories I'm working on with pi. Such a fascinating subject.
**Valerie:** You should have been present this weekend at the math-a-thon, Carl. The equations were simultaneously stimulating and challenging. My nearest guess is that they involved at least 30 percent of my brain's thinking capacity, which, as we all know, is much more than school requires!

*(Carl, Brian, and Valerie laugh.)*

**Brian:** Yes, I did so many equations, I became nauseous. It was wonderful, and further, it led to a hypothesis on what types of chemicals can be combined to create a cure for the overtaxation of one's brain.

**Carl:** Simply fabulous, chum! I regret that I was unable to join in the reverie. I was partaking of the wonderful computer-a-thon. Then I read *Scholar's Review*. I have received a subscription, you know.

**Brian:** Oh, yes, that is good, quite up-to-date on new and progressive science. Come to think of it, the computer I designed was featured at the computer-a-thon; it surpasses the best of the supercomputers. It far outranks anything coming out to the general public in the next ten years, and is more cutting-edge than even many of the top-secret government technologies. . . . But that is strictly between you and me, friend!

**Valerie:** Sadly, we must depart, or I will be late for my reception of the Nobel Prize in Physics. Or was it Chemistry? I will be receiving both; I am just diverting my brain power to unlock the global warming issue rather than remembering dates. Will you be viewing on the television, Carl?

**Carl:** Oh, I certainly would not miss it under other, more favorable circumstances, but I will be preparing my master's thesis today. I have always thought that by the age of twenty, I should have my master's degree, if not my PhD! I have found that my spare time has considerable space to accommodate such endeavors.

**Brian:** Stimulating. I will be interested in perusing your abstract. We must go. We will see you in Calculus 5.

**Carl:** So good to see you. And, Valerie, you might try asking Al Coholic about the global warming issue. Take care, guys!

**Valerie:** What? Al Coholic? Sure, hilarious joke! Good one, you quite nearly "got" me. See you!

*(Valerie and Brian leave.)*

**Carl:** Man, it's tough to be accepted and have friends. There's got to be an easier way! I'm not that athletic, pious, drug addicted, or smart. How can I find friends that fit *me?* How can I just be me? *(falls over from exhaustion)*

# Chapter Seven

# Building an Unsinkable Friendship

## The Art of Being a True Friend

## Overview

Central to any teen's existence is friendship. However, being surrounded by good friends and being a good friend are not necessarily typical of every teen's experience. This meeting identifies the important characteristics of being a friend. Additionally, it presents the evangelistic perspective on friendship, which has to include inviting others into a relationship with the perfect friend—Jesus Christ.

## Objectives

- To identify and practice the characteristics that make for good friendships
- To recognize and value Jesus Christ as our most reliable friend in life
- To invite or reinvite Jesus Christ to be our closest companion and best friend

## Scripture Passage

Faithful friends are a sturdy shelter:
   whoever finds one has found a treasure.
Faithful friends are beyond price;
   no amount can balance their worth.
Faithful friends are life-saving medicine;
   and those who fear the Lord will find them.
Those who fear the Lord direct their friendship aright,
   for as they are, so are their neighbors also.

(Sirach 6:14–17)

### Related Scripture Passages

- 1 Samuel 18:1–3
- Proverbs 11:13
- Proverbs 17:9
- Ecclesiastes 4:9–12
- Sirach 22:19–26

## Music Resources

- "Circle of Friends," performed by Point of Grace, from the CD *Life, Love and Other Mysteries*, Word Records, 2002.
- "A Friend Like U," performed by Geoff Moore and the Distance, from the CD *A Friend Like U*, Forefront Communications Group, 1992.
- "True Friend," performed by Twila Paris, from the CD *From Every Heart*, Star Song, 1988.
- "You've Got a Friend in Me," performed by Randy Newman, from the CD *Toy Story Soundtrack*, Walt Disney Records, 1999.

## Materials Needed and Preparation

☐ Gather the following items:
  ❏ Decorations for the gathering space (see the preparation step that follows this materials list)
  ❏ Cards cut from resource 14, "'A Friend Like U' Partners," one for each participant
  ❏ 6- to 8-inch stacks of newspaper, one for every eight participants
  ❏ Rolls of masking tape, one for every eight participants
  ❏ Three copies of resource 15, "Friendship Monologues"
  ❏ Newsprint and markers (optional)
  ❏ A flip chart
  ❏ A table
  ❏ A large candle and matches
  ❏ A picture of Jesus or a crucifix
  ❏ Two shallow trays filled with sand
  ❏ Two baskets filled with friendship bracelets, one bracelet for each participant
  ❏ Small candles or tea lights, one for each participant

❏ A recording of "In the Light," performed by DC Talk, from the CD *Jesus Freak*, Chordant Records, 1995

❏ A CD player or a tape player

❏ Refreshments

☐ The gathering space should be decorated to reinforce the theme of friendship. Here are some possibilities:

- On the walls post pictures of famous pairs and friends together (examples: Laurel and Hardy, Batman and Robin, Bert and Ernie, Mickey and Minnie, and Lucy and Ethel).

- Present an electronic slide show (for example, using PowerPoint) that includes pictures of friends together and Scripture passages about friendship.

- Display sinking "friend-ships" on which you have printed the words and phrases "gossip," "inability to keep a secret," "two-facedness," and "self-centeredness."

- Display floating "friend-ships" on which you have printed the words and phrases "trustworthiness," "authenticity," "friend focus," "love," "kindness," and "loyalty."

☐ Make enough copies of pages 1–4 of resource 14 to give you one pair of cards for every two participants. On the reverse of each sheet of cards, copy page 5 of the resource. Then cut out the cards as scored.

☐ Recruit three teen leaders or participants to assist with the friendship monologues. Provide each with a copy of resource 15 and ensure that the volunteers practice.

☐ Recruit a teen leader or a teen participant to give a 5-minute witness talk focusing on her or his experience of friendship. Ask the recruit to reflect on the following questions:

- In what kinds of situations have you learned how to be a friend?

- In what ways have others been friends to you? What characteristics or attributes of being a good friend have they illustrated?

- How have you learned about friendship from your own or others' mistakes? How have you grown in your ability to be a friend?

- What do you think are the most important aspects of being a friend? How have you lived those aspects in your friendships?

- Describe your friendship with Jesus Christ. In what ways has Jesus Christ been your best friend?

Meet with the teen a few days before the outreach, to review the talk's content and time frame and to provide encouragement.

☐ Consider noting the questions from the activity "Theme Introduction and Discussion" on newsprint.

☐ You will want to become very familiar with the presentation portion of this session in order to share the message rather than read it.

☐ Set up a prayer area that the teens can access during the prayer service. Include a table with a large candle in its center. Close to the candle, place a picture of Jesus or a crucifix. Using two shallow trays filled with sand, create placeholders for small candles on either side of the large candle. At the end of each tray, place a basket filled with friendship bracelets. (You can make the bracelets yourself, ask teens to make them, or purchase them from a craft store or from a Third World trading company.)

# Procedure

## Team Prayer (15 minutes before start)

Gather the ministry team together in order to get yourselves centered in prayer before the meeting. Begin by reading and reflecting on Sirach 6:14–17. Then pray for each activity and for those involved—both the ministers and the participants. Ask the Holy Spirit to speak through each element of the gathering and to draw the participants into a closer relationship with Jesus Christ, making him their closest companion and friend.

## Greeting (10 minutes before start)

Position your ministry team by the entrance doors and throughout the meeting room. Enthusiastically welcome each young person as he or she arrives. Create an attractive and appealing environment from the moment the teens enter. Make sure that no participant is standing alone. As you greet participants, quietly pray that they may leave the meeting filled with the peace of Christ.

## Introduction and Opening Prayer (5 minutes)

**1.** Welcome the group enthusiastically. Your level of excitement will help set the pace and attitude of the participants. Help make newcomers especially welcome by making special mention of them. Briefly introduce the theme of the gathering, saying something like this:

✦ Hello! My name is *(your name),* and I want to welcome you to *(your program's name).* Thank you for joining us this evening. I especially want to welcome any of you who are here for the first time. We are thrilled that you have joined us.

✦ This evening's meeting is called "Building an Unsinkable Friendship." We are going to look at what makes a good friend—and how to be one.

**2.** Invite the participants to join you in prayer, beginning with the sign of the cross. Offer a simple prayer that both invites God's presence and ties in the themes of the meeting, such as this one:

✦ Lord, we invite your presence in all that we do this evening. May your Holy Spirit speak to us and strengthen our ability to be real friends. Help us recognize you as our most trusted and reliable friend. May we grow in our friendship with you and all those around us. For this we pray. Amen.

## "A Friend Like U" Mixer (15 minutes)

**1.** Tell the participants that they will now have a chance to talk with a partner about their own experience with friendship. Give each participant a card cut from resource 14, making sure that you distribute both cards in each pair; if you have an uneven number of participants, give one card to a teen leader so that all the participants end up with a partner. Then instruct the participants to find the person whose card names a partner for their own. You may want to mention that the characters in the pairings may or may not be friends. For example, Mickey Mouse is the partner of Minnie Mouse, and the two are friends; however, Cain is the partner of Abel, and those two were not friends. Allow a minute or two for the partners to locate each other.

**2.** Invite the partners to sit down and exchange answers to the questions on the backs of their cards. Explain that they are to answer the questions as themselves, not as the characters on the other side of the cards. In other words, they are to give their partners their own full names, and so on.

## Friendship Fortress (15 minutes)

**1.** Divide the participants into teams of eight. Provide each team with a stack of newspaper and a roll of masking tape. Explain that the goal of this game is to build a newspaper fortress, with walls and a roof, that is self-supporting and can fully contain all the team members. Mention that the teams will have 10 minutes for building. Also inform the teams that awards will be given to the fortresses that are the sturdiest, the most welcoming, and the most creative.

**2.** Ask the participants if any of the instructions you have just given need to be clarified or repeated. Respond accordingly. Conduct the game as noted. Afterward, judge the structures and award the winners in each category.

## Friendship Monologues (10 minutes)

**1.** Introduce this portion of the gathering with these or similar words:
+ The Book of Sirach says, "Faithful friends are a sturdy shelter: whoever finds one has found a treasure" (6:14).
+ Friendship is important in our teenage years and in all of life. As wonderful as friendships can be, they also have the capacity to be disappointing.
+ The following monologues illustrate some of the struggles we might experience as we navigate the waters of friendships and other relationships.

**2.** Invite the volunteers to come forward and present the monologues from resource 15. Be sure to thank the actors at the completion of the monologues.

## Teen Witness Talk (5 minutes)

**1.** Introduce the teen leader or participant you have invited to share a witness talk, using these or similar words:
+ Friendships are an essential part of our lives. Sometimes we are disappointed in others, and sometimes we disappoint them. Being a good friend is something that we learn.
+ (Teen's name) is here to share his (or her) experience of friendship and what he (or she) has learned about having friends and being a friend.

**2.** At the conclusion of the witness talk, thank the person who has shared and offer any comments you think might help the group to move into the next portion of the gathering.

## Theme Introduction and Discussion (15 minutes)

Instruct the participants to gather into teams to discuss two or three of the following questions. You may wish to post these questions on newsprint.

- ✦ On a scale from 1 to 10 (with 1 being "Unimportant" and 10 being "Extremely Important"), how do you rate the importance of having good friends? Please explain your answer.
- ✦ The previous monologues and witness talk depict some of the difficulties with friendships. Do you find those experiences to be realistic? Please explain your answer.
- ✦ What do you see as the most significant barriers to being a true friend?
- ✦ What do you see as the most essential ingredients for true friendship?
- ✦ Describe the perfect friend.

## Keynote Presentation: A Real Friend (10 minutes)

Offer the following presentation in your own words:

- ✦ Think about all the friends you've ever had. Think about your best friend and what makes you care about her or him. Now think about a friend who has betrayed you. Reflect on how mad or hurt you have felt.
- ✦ Chances are you love your best friend because he or she has been there for you in good times and bad. This is the first person you call after you fight with your parents or break up with your boyfriend or girlfriend.
- ✦ Think of all the characteristics you want in a friend.

Pause for a moment. Ask the participants to give you characteristics of a true friend. Record them on a flip chart.

- ✦ So a good friend is *(list the characteristics written on the flip chart)*. Then be those things yourself. That will attract people of the same caliber. And if you find that you change into someone you don't like when you're around your friends, maybe it's time to think about whether you need those friends! Your friends should bring out the best in you. (The same goes for your boyfriends or girlfriends, by the way.) And, unlike your family, your friends are people you *get to choose*.

- You start to figure out this friend thing by being a real friend. Listen. Everyone in the world wants to feel that someone is really listening and cares. Be trustworthy. Don't gossip. Remember the old adage: If someone gossips *to* you, they'll gossip *about* you. If you really love your friends, you'll keep their confidence. You'll be there for them when they need you. You'll hang out with them and support them. And you'll be able to trust and depend on them in return.

- You know what to look for in a good friend; it's pretty obvious. Now can I make a suggestion? Try a friendship with Jesus Christ.

- I know, you're thinking, Please don't shove that "Jesus loves me, this I know, for the Bible tells me so" speech down my throat; I've been hearing it since kindergarten. So I won't. But let me just say this: One day you might feel that you don't have any friends. You might feel that you've been abandoned. Or maybe you'll just feel really lonely in spite of having a group of friends. Maybe that day won't come for years. Or maybe it's here right now, today.

- In that moment I want you to try something. I want you to try talking to Jesus Christ. Nothing fancy. Just tell him what's going on and how you feel. He'll always listen and care. He is the kind of friend who is *(point back at the characteristics listed on the flip chart)*.

- If you saw that your best friend was going to get run over by a bus, would you push her to safety and take the hit yourself? Maybe, if you were feeling really brave and had made your peace with God. But what if your friend's imminent death wasn't going to be quick and relatively painless? What if it was going to be slow and excruciatingly painful? Would you die for your best friend then?

- Jesus did. For you. For the person you're sitting next to. For everyone. All you have to do is turn to him and accept his love, and you'll have the best, most devoted friend you could ever ask for.

Darken the room to create a prayerful atmosphere, and move right into the closing prayer, as though the talk is actually continuing.

## Closing Prayer: In the Light (10 minutes)

**1.** Invite the participants to gather around the prayer table. Provide each with a small candle or a tea light, and light the large candle. Tell the teens the following things in your own words:

✦ I will be playing a song. During the song you are invited to approach the prayer table one at a time and light your candles and place them in the sand. As you light your candles, do one or both of these things:
  ◇ Offer a prayer of gratitude for a friend or for the gift of friendship.
  ◇ Pray for a deeper friendship with Jesus Christ.
✦ You should do all this in complete silence. Once you have offered your silent prayer, you may take a friendship bracelet from the basket and return to your seat to listen to the remainder of the song.

**2.** Once everyone understands the ritual, begin playing the song "In the Light" and invite a participant to lead off.

## Refreshments (15 minutes)

Young people will stick around after the meeting if there is something to eat. Use this postgathering follow-up time to further establish relationships with teens, find out what they thought of the session, and continue to share your faith one-on-one. Remember: the best large-group evangelization does not stand solely on its program but is undergirded by a web of relationships that reinforce the evangelistic message interpersonally.

# "A Friend Like U" Partners

| | |
|---|---|
| Abbott | Costello |
| Adam | Eve |
| Batman | Robin |
| Sonny | Cher |
| Laurel | Hardy |
| Lois | Clark |
| Bonnie | Clyde |
| Simon | Garfunkel |
| Smokey | The Bandit |

**Resource 14:** Permission to reproduce is granted. © 2004 by Cultivation Ministries.

| | |
|---|---|
| Jack | Jill |
| Mickey | Minnie |
| Cain | Abel |
| David | Goliath |
| Laverne | Shirley |
| Fred | Wilma |
| Barney | Betty |
| Siegfried | Roy |
| The Lone Ranger | Tonto |
| Homer | Marge |

| | |
|---|---|
| Snow White | The Seven Dwarves |
| Thelma | Louise |
| Beauty | The Beast |
| Bert | Ernie |
| Cinderella | Prince Charming |
| John Lennon | Yoko Ono |
| Romeo | Juliet |
| Brooks | Dunn |
| Mork | Mindy |
| Shaggy | Scooby-Doo |

| The Mamas | The Papas |
|-----------|-----------|
| Desi | Lucy |
| Samson | Delilah |
| Dr. Jekyll | Mr. Hyde |
| Mary | Joseph |
| Sylvester | Tweety |
| Tom | Jerry |
| Penn | Teller |
| Wally | The Beaver |
| Barnum | Bailey |

What is your full name?
What do you like most
  about your best friend?
What makes you a good friend?

What is your full name?
What do you like most
  about your best friend?
What makes you a good friend?

What is your full name?
What do you like most
  about your best friend?
What makes you a good friend?

What is your full name?
What do you like most
  about your best friend?
What makes you a good friend?

What is your full name?
What do you like most
  about your best friend?
What makes you a good friend?

What is your full name?
What do you like most
  about your best friend?
What makes you a good friend?

What is your full name?
What do you like most
  about your best friend?
What makes you a good friend?

What is your full name?
What do you like most
  about your best friend?
What makes you a good friend?

What is your full name?
What do you like most
  about your best friend?
What makes you a good friend?

What is your full name?
What do you like most
  about your best friend?
What makes you a good friend?

What is your full name?
What do you like most
  about your best friend?
What makes you a good friend?

What is your full name?
What do you like most
  about your best friend?
What makes you a good friend?

What is your full name?
What do you like most
  about your best friend?
What makes you a good friend?

What is your full name?
What do you like most
  about your best friend?
What makes you a good friend?

What is your full name?
What do you like most
  about your best friend?
What makes you a good friend?

What is your full name?
What do you like most
  about your best friend?
What makes you a good friend?

What is your full name?
What do you like most
  about your best friend?
What makes you a good friend?

What is your full name?
What do you like most
  about your best friend?
What makes you a good friend?

What is your full name?
What do you like most
  about your best friend?
What makes you a good friend?

What is your full name?
What do you like most
  about your best friend?
What makes you a good friend?

# Friendship Monologues

## Monologue 1

Hi. My name is Egan. Egan Knoor. Cole is one of my neighbors. Oh, there he is now. *(looking in a direction and waving)* Hi, Cole . . . *(words trail in disappointment at not being noticed; head hangs)*

We've known each other since we were in first grade, when Cole moved in a couple of houses down from mine. We were best friends until sixth grade. We did everything together—sleepovers, parties, sports—just everything.

He was always a better athlete, but it didn't matter when we were young, we were always on the same side. Things changed in high school. Cole got cool, or at least he now hangs around people who are cool. Funny, that's about the only thing that's changed—that and his attitude.

Around the neighborhood, I'm a person. He'll say hi and talk with me. Around his friends, I'm not a person. He pretends he doesn't see me. I guess I am a risk to his reputation, so he ignores me in public. It's funny how saying hi to me in public can cost Cole his image. *(hanging head)* Not really. It's not funny. It hurts.

## Monologue 2

I am a star—a celebrity of sorts. You're wondering why I am not happy. Doesn't everyone want to be famous? Doesn't everyone want to be recognized and known by the public?

You see, sometimes my heart is exploding. I have always wanted to have a friend I could share my thoughts, feelings, and dreams with. A friend who's a safe harbor—a person I can trust. My friend Cherie was that person. Around her I could be me. The more I trusted her, the more I opened my heart. Last night I shared with her the things closest to my heart.

It felt good to share what was deeply buried. What a wonderful release. I felt understood and not like I was the only one who had these feelings. I went home feeling like I had the friend I always wanted.

This morning I feel nauseous. I am famous—at least at my school. I shared some intimate and personal feelings with Cherie, and she published the information. She told a friend, and that friend told others, and others told others. I am the topic of conversation of even those who don't know me. I am a "celebrity." A reluctant "star."

I feel exposed, naked, and vulnerable. I wish I was never born. I feel embarrassed and betrayed. I'll never trust another person again.

    **Resource 15:** Permission to reproduce is granted. © 2004 by Cultivation Ministries.

## Monologue 3

I don't even like my friends. Seriously, I know that sounds weird, but I don't. I can't wait to go away to college and get away from them. I won't miss them. There's nothing to miss.

I haven't found a true friend. You know, the kind of friend you read about in books—the one who is always there for you, the one you feel free enough to share anything with, the friend who would do anything for you. I haven't found anyone who even slightly resembles that.

My so-called best friend, Donna, who I have known since the first grade, doesn't really care about me. In fact last year she practically forgot about my birthday. She's never cared about me as much as I have cared about her. Once, in junior high, she found something better to do than hang out with me, so she told me she had to walk her dog. I found out later what she really did. By lying she thought she would avoid hurting me. Instead she multiplied my pain and subtracted my trust.

In high school she found a new group of friends who replaced me until she got sick of them. Then she discovered boys. I don't think we've had a meaningful conversation since. She calls me in between boyfriends.

Then there's my so-called friend Kathy. She acts likes she really cares about me, but concealed behind the words is an ulterior motive. It's like everything she says to me is about impressing someone else who might be listening—someone more important, more popular. I am not a real person with real feelings.

Last year all my friends had a date for a dance except me. Word was out that one of the guys in our class was going to ask me. I would like to have gone with him. Kathy already had a date and knew he was thinking about asking me, but decided she liked him and threw herself all over him. I could hardly get a word in. Needless to say I sat home the night of the dance. He never asked me. He didn't think I was interested. My so-called friend, who already had a date, took my only opportunity. Whatever happened to loyalty to a friend? The only loyalty I see is to self.

Maybe real friendship is only fiction. Most people I know are pretty much about themselves. When I want friendship, I guess I'll go to the library and take out a book.

# Chapter Eight

# Slamming the Door on Backseat Romance

## Understanding God's Plan for Sexuality

## Overview

Teens are immersed in a culture that often expects them to have premarital sex. This session explores the virtue of chastity and the wisdom of waiting until marriage before forming sexual relationships. The meeting examines why God's plan for sex inside of marriage makes great sense, and it highlights a practical plan for practicing chastity.

Note: In this session you must be pastorally sensitive to many different experiences of teens. Statistics suggest that some of your participants will have already had sexual relations. Several may have been sexually molested. Some will perceive that they are sexually inactive by "default" and feel that if they were only more attractive or popular, they would have already had sex. Some will have an active commitment to chastity out of a conviction that they wish to follow God's plan for them. You need to be prepared to address those different experiences. It is wise to have available counseling referral resources as well as times and locations for upcoming celebrations of the sacrament of Penance and Reconciliation.

## Objectives

- To clearly understand God's plan for sex and dating as revealed in the teaching of the Catholic Church
- To understand how God's plan is given in love to protect us from harm emotionally, physically, and spiritually

## Scripture Passage

Shun fornication. Every sin that a person commits is outside the body; but the fornicator sins against the body itself. Or do you not know that your body is a temple of the Holy Spirit, within you, which you have from God and that you are not your own? For you were bought at a price; therefore glorify God in your body. (1 Corinthians 6:18)

## Music Resources

- "A Girl Named World," performed by Ambassadors (Rap), from the CD *Christology in Laymen's Terms*, DMG, 2000.
- "Give Me One Reason," performed by Zoe Girl, from the CD *Zoe Girl*, Sparrow Records, 2000.
- "I Am the One," performed by Out of Eden, from the CD *This Is Your Life*, Gotee Records, 2002.
- "Wait for Me," performed by Rebecca St. James, from the CD *Transform,* ForeFront/Emd Records, 2000.

## Materials Needed and Preparation

☐ Gather the following items:
- ❏ Decorations for the gathering space (see the preparation step that follows this materials list)
- ❏ An assortment of Hershey's Hugs and Kisses (plain and almond), five or six for each participant
- ❏ Plastic sandwich bags, one for each participant
- ❏ One large almond Hershey's Kiss or a bag of almond Hershey's Kisses (optional)
- ❏ Masking tape
- ❏ A rope or a sheet
- ❏ A watch, clock, or timer that marks seconds
- ❏ Three copies of resource 16, "'Odd Man Out' Skit"
- ❏ Props for the skit on resource 16 (listed on the resource)
- ❏ Newsprint and a marker (optional)
- ❏ Resource 17, "Chastity Pledge Cards"
- ❏ A selection from this session's "Music Resources" section
- ❏ A CD player or a tape player
- ❏ Refreshments

☐ The meeting room should be decorated to reinforce the theme that God's plan for dating and sex is better than the lies conveyed by the media and our culture. Here is one possibility:

## Related Scripture Passages

- Jeremiah 29:11
- Matthew 15:18–19
- Ephesians 5:3–7
- Colossians 3:5

- Decorate half of the meeting or stage area with glittery gold paper or fabric. In large letters, paint or write on the gold background the Scripture verse from Jeremiah 29:11. Use bright lights on this side of the area.

  Decorate the other half of the meeting or stage area with red paper or fabric. From teen magazines cut pictures or statements that typify the false messages our culture sends about teen sexuality. This side of the area should be darker and less attractive than the gold side.

  In the midpoint of the meeting or stage area, the red and gold papers or fabrics should meet. Bridging them, position a large image of Jesus. Underneath that image, write in large letters the Scripture passage from 1 John 1:9 or from 2 Corinthians 5:17.

☐ To prepare for the "Be Careful Whom You Kiss" mixer, put five or six Hershey's Hugs and Kisses, both plain and almond, into each sandwich bag. Also ask several teen leaders to serve as Hug-and-Kiss stealers; you will need one stealer for every ten participants. Explain that the stealers are to keep their identities a secret. During the mixer they will take all the Hugs and Kisses away from every fifth person who asks them for a Hug or a Kiss. They are the only ones who will be able to take more than one Hug or Kiss at a time. They should hide some of their stolen Hugs and Kisses in their pockets so that it will not be obvious that they are stealers.

☐ For the activity "Hormone Tug-of-War," use masking tape to make a centerline in your meeting area. If you are using a small room, you may need help clearing space for the game.

☐ Recruit three teen leaders or participants to assist with the skit on resource 16. Provide each with a copy of the resource and ensure that the volunteers practice the skit.

☐ Recruit a teen leader or a teen participant to give a 5-minute witness talk about how he or she is incorporating God's plan for chastity in his or her life. To help the recruit prepare, offer the following questions for reflection:

- What does God have to do with how I approach dating and sex?
- What are some practical things I do to stay within God's plan for dating and saving sex until marriage?
- What has my own experience or that of someone close to me taught me about why waiting until marriage to have sex is part of God's loving plan for us?

Meet with the teen a few days before the outreach, to review the content and time frame of the talk and to provide encouragement.

☐ Consider noting the questions from the activity "Theme Introduction and Discussion" on newsprint.

☐ You will want to become very familiar with the presentation portion of this session in order to share the message rather than read it.

☐ Copy pages 1 and 2 of resource 17 back-to-back, so that the pledges appear on one side of a sheet of paper, and the Bible verses appear on the other side. Cut out the resulting cards as scored. You will need one card for each participant.

## Procedure

### Team Prayer (15 minutes before start)

Gather the ministry team together in order to get yourselves centered in prayer before the meeting. Begin by reading and reflecting on 1 Timothy 4:12,16. Then pray for each activity and for those involved—both the ministers and the participants. As a team thank God for the opportunity to serve him and ask for the grace to be chaste in your thoughts, speech, and actions. Pray that the Holy Spirit will work through this outreach to speak truth to each person's heart and to convince each person that God's plan of saving sex for marriage is truly the best way to approach the issue of dating and sex.

### Greeting (10 minutes before start)

Position your ministry team by the entrance doors and throughout the meeting room. Enthusiastically welcome each young person as he or she arrives. Create an attractive and appealing environment from the moment teens get there. Make sure that no participant is standing alone. As you greet the participants, quietly pray that they may leave the meeting filled with the peace of Christ.

### Introduction and Opening Prayer (5 minutes)

**1.** Welcome the group enthusiastically. Your level of excitement will help set the pace and attitude of the participants. Help make newcomers especially welcome by making special mention of them. Briefly introduce the theme of the gathering, saying something like this:

- Hello! My name is *(your name)*, and I want to welcome you to *(your program's name)*. Thank you for joining us this evening. I especially want to welcome any of you who are here for the first time. We are thrilled that you have joined us.
- This evening's meeting is titled "Slamming the Door on Backseat Romance." We are going to look at God's plan for dating and sex.

**2.** Invite the participants to join you in prayer, beginning with the sign of the cross. Say a simple prayer that both invites God's presence and ties in the theme. The following words offer an example:

- Lord, we ask you to be present with us this evening. Please help us to understand your plan for dating and sex. Let the truth of your love for us be clear, and help us to trust in your good plan. We ask this in Jesus's name.

## "Be Careful Whom You Kiss" Mixer (10 minutes)

**1.** Distribute the sandwich bags of Hugs and Kisses that you created before the session. Then offer the following instructions and information:

- All of you were given Hershey's Hugs and Kisses. The gold Kisses are the most valuable.
- Each of you will approach another person and say: "Hello, my name is *(your name)*. Do you have a Hug or a Kiss for me?"
- The other person must give you one of her or his Hershey's Hugs or Kisses, trying to avoid giving away any gold Kisses.
- If you have only gold Kisses, you must give those away.
- Beware that there are Hug-and-Kiss stealers among you. When every fifth person asks a Hug-and-Kiss stealer for a kiss, the stealer will say, "No, but I will take all your Hugs and Kisses." If that happens to you, then you must give the stealer all your Hugs and Kisses, and you are out of the game.
- The identities of the stealers are, of course, a secret. If you get your Hugs and Kisses stolen, do not reveal who the stealer is.

Ask the participants if any of the instructions you have just given need to be clarified or repeated, and respond accordingly.

**2.** Play the game for about 8 minutes, then ask the remaining players (excluding the Hug-and-Kiss stealers) to count their gold Hershey's Kisses. The player with the most gold Kisses at the end of the game is the winner. You may wish to award the winner a large gold Kiss or a bag of gold Kisses.

**3.** Explain that life is similar to this game. Say something like this:

✦ The gold Kisses are the most valuable, and they represent our chastity and love. You don't want to give away your chastity or your love to just anyone. You must be careful, or you can lose everything, including the valuable gift of your virginity. We must not casually give ourselves away, or we will be out of the game, empty-handed and disappointed, and we will have lost much more than a bag of chocolate Hugs and Kisses!

## Hormone Tug-of-War (10 minutes)

**1.** Ask for ten to twenty volunteers. Divide the volunteers in half to create two teams. Ask one team to line up on one side of the centerline you created with masking tape, and the other team to line up on the opposite side. Give each team one end of a rope or a sheet.

**2.** Designate one team the Hormones and the other the Conscience. Ask for two more volunteers to coach the teams. Instruct the Hormones' coach to shout common messages such as: "You know you love him, and it's not really a big deal!" "Everyone does it, and nothing happens to them!" "Others expect you to do it!" and "You'll be made fun of if you're the only one who hasn't gone all the way!"

Direct the Conscience's coach to shout positive messages such as: "God has a great plan for you!" "Waiting is worth it!" "It's hard, but you can do it!" and "You are worth saving for someone special!"

Explain that the rest of the participants are to cheer for one of the teams.

**3.** Tell everyone that the game will be played for 2 minutes, and the winner will be whichever team has pulled the other over the line or closest to the line when you call time.

Ask the participants if any of the instructions you have just given need to be clarified or repeated. Respond accordingly. Conduct the game as noted.

**4.** After 2 minutes call the game and applaud the winner. Offer the following comments in your own words:

✦ This game is similar to our experience with sex. We feel the tug between our strong emotions and drives, and what we know is best for us in the long run. We are pulled one way and then the next. But there is one difference: we have a choice about which side of the line we end up on. We can choose to avoid crossing the line by not getting too close to it, and we can also choose what messages we put in our minds.

## "Odd Man Out" Skit (10 minutes)

**1.** Introduce this activity with these or similar words:

✦ The two games we've played have shown us that our chastity and love are valuable and are sources of internal conflict. From our discussions of these games, we have learned that we have choices—about how we give our love away and about what "voices" we listen to concerning the place of sex and dating in our lives.

✦ The fact is, unless we decide now what is right for us and how we are going to live out our beliefs, we'll easily be swayed by the media and culture around us. Let's see what choices Andy, Eric, and Mike have made in their lives.

**2.** Invite the three volunteers to come forward and present the skit from resource 16. Be sure to thank the actors at the completion of the skit.

## Teen Witness Talk (5 minutes)

**1.** Introduce the teen leader or participant you have invited to share a witness talk, using these or similar words:

✦ We saw how Andy, Eric, and Mike have dealt with the issue of dating and sex in their lives. *(Teen witness's name)* is going to share with us some thoughts about that area in his (or her) life.

**2.** At the conclusion of the talk, thank the person who has shared and offer any comments you think might help the group to move into the next portion of the gathering.

## Theme Introduction and Discussion (10 minutes)

Instruct the participants to gather into teams to discuss two or three of the following questions. You may wish to post these questions on newsprint.

✦ Where does the strongest pressure to have sex before marriage come from? How is that pressure the same for guys and girls? How does it differ?

✦ Which of the possible negative consequences of engaging in premarital sex seems the worst to you? Why?

✦ Some "experts" say that abstinence is unrealistic for teens. Do you agree or disagree? Please explain your reasoning.

✦ Some say that the greatest gift one can give a spouse is one's virginity. Do you agree or disagree? Please explain your reasoning.

✦ What are the advantages of deciding what is or isn't acceptable for you before you find yourself in a particular dating situation?

## Keynote Presentation: Why Wait? (15 minutes)

Offer the following presentation in your own words:

✦ During spring break a young couple in Chicago decided to surprise their five small children with a trip to Walt Disney World in Florida.

They woke the kids one morning to a packed van and a mystery trip. At first, of course, the children thought they were going to Cleveland to see their grandparents. As they drove, they'd even point out scenery they thought they recalled from their many previous trips to Ohio.

After a full day of driving, the family stopped at a motel in Tennessee. The fun was starting to wear off. As they approached Atlanta the next morning, the children's patience was—shall we say—wearing thin.

The parents had planned this in the spirit of fun. What they got instead was an angry mob in the backseats, stamping their feet and chanting: "CLEVE-land! CLEVE-land! CLEVE-land!" The youngsters weren't impressed with the direction they were heading, and began to question their mom and dad's ability to navigate. At that moment, nothing in their wildest dreams could possibly be better than Cleveland.

Trying to avert disaster, Mom gave them the map. She told them to follow the road they were on, going south. Before long, it dawned on them that they were headed for Florida. And when they finally guessed that they were going to Disney World, all was forgiven.

Clearly Mom and Dad wanted to fulfill the dream of their children's hearts. They had their kids' best interests in mind. Indeed the trip did turn out to be a blast for each of the children—but the journey was a troubled one. For a moment there, the kids didn't trust their parents' intentions.

✦ Much like those children, we sometimes don't know where God is taking us, and we begin to question his wisdom. I find that especially true in the area of dating and sexual relationships.

✦ God wants to protect us from any harm that can come our way. As any good father, God does not want us to enter into situations or circumstances that can prove dangerous to our welfare. Like any good parent, God has established boundaries that are concrete expressions of his love.

✦ What does God want to protect us from? First, God wants to guard us from the *emotional* and *physical* pain that can accompany sex outside a marital commitment. As a result of sexual intercourse, couples experience a powerful emotional attachment called bonding. The closeness and connectedness of bonding helps draw a couple together. Within the context of a committed marital love, this works wonderfully.

✦ Outside marriage, however, the bonding that results from intercourse has a negative impact. Breakups become extremely painful. Sexual bonds are not severed without substantial emotional trauma. Our bodies and emotional makeup were designed for one partner.

✦ We have been well conditioned to an "anything goes" sexual morality by the television shows and movies we have seen over the years. The message is convincing and even appealing. The problem is, it's only great fiction. It doesn't work in real life.

✦ Somehow the media have been silent about the painful reality faced by those who imitate what they see in countless television episodes. Many people struggle agonizingly with sexual mistakes for years. Some even pay for those mistakes with their lives. Disentangling ourselves from the deceptive and destructive lies of the media is a difficult challenge.

✦ Second, God wants to protect us from the *spiritual* pain of sex outside marriage. When we choose to follow our own way and live independently of God, we close off our relationship with him. Out of love and respect, God gives us that freedom of choice.

✦ Because sex outside marriage is a sin, it can construct a barrier in our relationship with God. That is one dangerous aspect of sin.

✦ You might ask: "Whose wisdom will I trust to guide and navigate me through life? I can't even predict what will happen tomorrow! Should I trust God, who is omniscient (all-knowing), omnipresent (everywhere), omnipotent (all-powerful), and eternal (forever)?" The choice is your plan or God's plan—Cleveland or Disney World.

✦ A marriage built on respect, love, and unselfishness, demonstrated through waiting, has the ingredients for a fulfilling and lasting relationship.

✦ Some of us may have already made some mistakes sexually in the past. Does that mean we are doomed in the future? No. Our God is a God of hope. God is happy to forgive, heal, and restore. What matters now is the future we begin to build today.

✦ Plenty of young people may agree with all that I say, yet somehow find themselves compromising what they know is right. For most of them, their actions will detour from their convictions because they lack a plan to live by. A practical plan to abide by daily is essential. Here are some suggestions for developing one:

   ◇ Give God control over whom you date and what you do on a date. Follow God's guidelines and directives as given through the Bible and Church teaching.

   ◇ Set your limits and tenaciously stick by them. Our bodies were never meant to build sexual steam and then slam to a stop right before intercourse. Sooner or later either your brakes will give out or you will fail to apply them. Set high standards that keep you safe from losing control.

   ◇ Share with a significant person in your life your standards and commitment to chastity. Make your conduct accountable to that person.

- ◇ It is best not to put yourself in a relationship with another person who is not committed to Christ and waiting until marriage. The pressure of someone you are emotionally involved with can prove to be too much.
- ◇ Avoid tempting circumstances. Don't put yourself in an environment that can reduce your defenses. Spending significant amounts of time at your girl-friend's home when her parents are gone can be dangerous. Make planned and intelligent choices about where you are going to go and what you are going to do when you are together. Additionally, don't drink or use drugs. Drinking and using drugs like Ecstasy can reduce inhibitions, causing a person to do things he or she would otherwise never consider.
- ◇ Pray each day for God's strength to live out his desire for your life. If you ask God, he will gladly provide you with the strength to carry out his will.
- ✦ Committing ourselves to God and to his plan for our sexuality may not be easy in today's culture. Our friends may not understand or approve. But we can be assured that when we are obedient to God, he will protect us from the negative consequences of premarital sex, and we will truly "have life, and have it abundantly" (John 10:10).
- ✦ And, by the way, if you have second thoughts during the journey, and find yourself yelling "CLEVE-land! CLEVE-land! CLEVE-land!" look to see if God isn't saying, "My child, if I took you there, you'd miss Disney World."

Move right into the closing prayer, as though the talk is actually continuing.

## Closing Prayer: Chastity Pledge (10 minutes)

**1.** Invite the participants to think about what they have heard today, and what it means to them. You could say something like this:

- ✦ Some of you have already experienced the emotional, physical, and spiritual pain that I've described. You feel that you've already lost something that you can never get back. God wants you to know that he loves you, no matter what. God wants to restore the gift of chastity to you and to heal you.

- Some of you are sexually active right now and don't see anything wrong with that because you feel that you genuinely love your girlfriend or boyfriend. But the most loving thing you can do for the person you are dating is to stop having sex. Unless you are ready for marriage and the very real possibility of having children, then this is not the time for sex. Because sex outside marriage is outside God's plan for you, it is a sin and it will have negative consequences in your relationship with your girlfriend or boyfriend. It places a barrier between you and God and the good plan God has for you and this other person. God wants you to know that he loves you no matter what. God wants to restore the gift of chastity to you and to heal you.

- Some of you have not willingly given away your virginity but it has been violently taken from you through the terrible acts of another. Jesus Christ's heart breaks for you. You have not sinned—it is not your fault. God wants you to know that he loves you no matter what. He wants to hold you in his loving arms, restore the gift of chastity to you, and heal you.

- Some of you have made the choice to remain chaste. You have sought to follow God in this area of your lives and have made conscious choices about what you watch, what you listen to, whom you hang around with, and whom, how, and if you date. Jesus Christ wants you to know that he is pleased with your choice. God promises to help you; God loves you and wants to strengthen you.

- No matter where you are coming from, Jesus Christ is here for you.

**2.** Distribute the pledge cards you created from resource 17. Then continue by noting the following ideas in your own words:

- We have provided each of you with a pledge card. We are going to take some time alone with God and then pray together.

**3.** Invite the participants to spread out and find a quiet place to sit in the room. Invite them to listen to the music you have selected. At the end of the song, say the following prayer:

- Lord Jesus, we believe that you are here, right now, for each of us. You know where we are, where we have been, and where we are going in our lives. Please forgive us for the times that we have purposely walked away from you. Please restore to each of us the precious gift of being able to give ourselves sexually to our husbands or wives. Please heal us if we have been hurt physically, emotionally, or spiritually in a sexual way. Help us to take the next right step in living out your plan for us. Thank you, Lord Jesus, for loving us and helping each of us. Amen.

## Refreshments (15 minutes)

Young people will stick around after the meeting if there is something to eat. Use this postgathering follow-up time to further establish relationships with teens, find out what they thought of the session, and continue to share your faith one-on-one. Remember: the best large-group evangelization does not stand solely on its program but is undergirded by a web of relationships that reinforce the evangelistic message interpersonally.

# "Odd Man Out" Skit

## Cast

- Andy
- Eric
- Mike

## Props

- A couch
- Stairs

## Script

*(The scene opens in the basement of Andy's house, with a couch facing the crowd and an assumed, but not actually present, television. Andy is seated, supposedly watching a game, when his friends Eric and Mike enter, descending the stairs to the left. They greet Andy as they sit down on the couch beside him.)*

**Mike and Eric:** *(giving high fives and punching Andy's arm)* Hey brotha! What's up, man? How you doin'? How's the game?

**Andy:** We're behind by four. But we'll bring it back, I'm sure. Always do fourth quarter. You guys are late; what was the holdup?

**Mike:** *(rolls his eyes and glances over at Eric)* We couldn't get away from Eric's house 'cuz his *girlfriend (in a singsong)* wouldn't let him off the phone. Man, that girl is a DRAG! I swear I can hear the whip crack every time he answers the phone.

**Andy:** *(laughs)*

**Eric:** Aw, shut up, man! I had to get her off my case.

**Andy:** What's she all riled up about THIS time?

**Eric:** She's already bugging me about prom when it's months away.

**Mike:** *(easily distracted, with eyes on the game)* Oh, oh, oh, IT'S GOOD! *(stands to do a victory dance)* Man, are you guys even watching? *(flops back onto the couch, exasperated)* That was the best touchdown we've had all season. Seventy yards, and you two miss it because you're too busy talking about what, girls? Eric, you just need to dump her like a bad habit. That or get over it. All girls do crazy things like ask about dances months before they happen, or go to the bathroom in groups. Why DO they DO that? Guys don't go to the bathroom in groups!

**Eric and Andy:** *(nod in agreement)*

**Andy:** The world may never know, my friend, the world may never know.

**Eric and Mike:** *(nod in solemn agreement)*

**Mike:** *(with a sly grin)* Anyway, Eric . . . so, how far you got with her?

**Andy:** *(sounding offended for his friend)* What? Why're you askin' that?

**Mike:** *(with a smile)* It's a fair question. C'mon, Eric, 'fess up.

**Eric:** *(looks perturbed and slightly mad)* It's none of your business, man.

**Mike:** Aw, c'mon; you're among friends here! *(gestures widely around the room, as though indicating invisible confidants who fill the basement, in addition to the three friends)*

**Andy:** *(under his breath)* Listen, Mike, that ain't cool. Leave him alone.

**Mike:** What's the DEAL!? It was a simple question. Don't tell me you're going to go off on me again like last time, Andy, with all that *(adopts a nasally tone)* "this is what the Bible says and this is what Jesus says" bull!

**Resource 16:** Permission to reproduce is granted. © 2004 by Cultivation Ministries.

*(Andy is about to respond hotly, but Eric cuts him off.)*

**Eric:** You know what, Mike? All this time I've let you make fun of Andy for having morals and respecting women like they're more than just pieces of meat to be had. Okay, so Vanessa is a little uptight about some stuff, and yeah, she even occasionally bugs me. But you know what? I've seen too many people get messed up by NOT following Andy's *(imitates Mike's snide nasally voice)* "Jesus bull." Diseases, pregnancies, dropping out of high school to support a kid, the way everyone looks at you or her when they know you're pregnant.

*(Mike tries to butt in, but Andy beats him to it.)*

**Andy:** God does have a way he wants us to do stuff. Not just to beat rules down on us, but for our own good. You think God is just some cop up in heaven trying to make sure no one has any fun?

**Mike:** *(putting his hands up in protest)* Whoa! All I was saying was—

**Eric:** *(cuts in)* That girls ain't nothin' but the flavor of the week. But know what? Whether or not I believe in Andy's God or in morals or whatever, he's got a point. I love Vanessa, and I'm not going to do anything with her more than kiss.

**Andy:** *(pauses before interjecting quietly)* Listen, I'm not asking either of you to believe in God or Jesus or anything. All I'm saying is that I believe in God, that he believes in you, and that honestly, if you follow his plan, everything works out better. You don't ever have to worry about getting nasty diseases or getting a girl pregnant. And even in the best-case scenario, where none of that happens, you can emotionally scar someone, and I've been hurt myself too many times to want to let that happen to someone else.

*(There is silence for a moment as everyone reflects on what was just said.)*

**Mike:** Listen, Eric, I'm sorry, man—

**Eric:** Naw, it's alright, bro. No biggie. Just lay off Vanessa, okay? She means a lot to me.

**Andy:** Sorry to lay into you like that, Mike. But you know how I am.

**Mike:** Yeah, whatever, it's okay.

*(Silence lies between the friends as they consider what just occurred.)*

# Chastity Pledge Cards

I choose to take actions that will reflect my love for, respect for, and commitment to God, my potential future spouse, and myself. With God's help I place (or re-place) my chastity in God's loving hands, saving sex for marriage.

I choose to take actions that will reflect my love for, respect for, and commitment to God, my potential future spouse, and myself. With God's help I place (or re-place) my chastity in God's loving hands, saving sex for marriage.

I choose to take actions that will reflect my love for, respect for, and commitment to God, my potential future spouse, and myself. With God's help I place (or re-place) my chastity in God's loving hands, saving sex for marriage.

I choose to take actions that will reflect my love for, respect for, and commitment to God, my potential future spouse, and myself. With God's help I place (or re-place) my chastity in God's loving hands, saving sex for marriage.

I choose to take actions that will reflect my love for, respect for, and commitment to God, my potential future spouse, and myself. With God's help I place (or re-place) my chastity in God's loving hands, saving sex for marriage.

I choose to take actions that will reflect my love for, respect for, and commitment to God, my potential future spouse, and myself. With God's help I place (or re-place) my chastity in God's loving hands, saving sex for marriage.

I choose to take actions that will reflect my love for, respect for, and commitment to God, my potential future spouse, and myself. With God's help I place (or re-place) my chastity in God's loving hands, saving sex for marriage.

I choose to take actions that will reflect my love for, respect for, and commitment to God, my potential future spouse, and myself. With God's help I place (or re-place) my chastity in God's loving hands, saving sex for marriage.

For surely I know the plans I have for you, says the Lord, plans for your welfare and not for harm, to give you a future with hope. (Jeremiah 29:11)

For surely I know the plans I have for you, says the Lord, plans for your welfare and not for harm, to give you a future with hope. (Jeremiah 29:11)

For surely I know the plans I have for you, says the Lord, plans for your welfare and not for harm, to give you a future with hope. (Jeremiah 29:11)

For surely I know the plans I have for you, says the Lord, plans for your welfare and not for harm, to give you a future with hope. (Jeremiah 29:11)

For surely I know the plans I have for you, says the Lord, plans for your welfare and not for harm, to give you a future with hope. (Jeremiah 29:11)

For surely I know the plans I have for you, says the Lord, plans for your welfare and not for harm, to give you a future with hope. (Jeremiah 29:11)

For surely I know the plans I have for you, says the Lord, plans for your welfare and not for harm, to give you a future with hope. (Jeremiah 29:11)

For surely I know the plans I have for you, says the Lord, plans for your welfare and not for harm, to give you a future with hope. (Jeremiah 29:11)

# Chapter Nine

# The Birth of a New Self-Worth

## Taking to Heart
## God's Real Love for Us

### Overview

We live in a "cosmetic culture," and therefore much of how we feel about ourselves is often based on how we evaluate our looks and bodies. In this session the participants explore the tenets of the cosmetic culture and evaluate them in the light of the Scriptures. Additionally, the participants are challenged to find a more accurate measure of their self-worth that is based on the reliable facts of our faith, that is, that the Father created us, the Son died for us, and the Holy Spirit lives within us.

### Objectives

- To recognize the fallacy of basing self-worth on body image
- To value how God sees us as the only true standard of our self-worth
- To make the sign of the cross a regular reminder of our worth in God's eyes

### Themes
- Self-worth and self-image
- Appearance

### Schedule
- Pregathering Hospitality
  - Team Prayer
    (15 minutes before start)
  - Greeting
    (10 minutes before start)
- Welcome
  - Introduction
    (5 minutes)
  - Opening Prayer
    (5 minutes)
  - Connection Mixer
    (25 minutes)
- Warm-Up
  - Fashion Flair Competition (10 minutes)
- Message
  - "Whata Ya Doin'?" Skit (10 minutes)
  - Teen Witness Talk
    (5 minutes)
  - Theme Introduction and Discussion
    (10 minutes)
  - Keynote Presentation: The Sign of Self-Worth (15 minutes)
- Closure
  - Closing Prayer:
    A Unique Gift
    (10 minutes)
- Postgathering Follow-Up
  - Refreshments
    (15 minutes)

## Scripture Passage

But the LORD said to Samuel, "Do not look on his appearance or on the height of his stature. Because I have rejected him; for the LORD does not see as mortals see; they look on the outward appearance, but the LORD looks on the heart." (1 Samuel 16:7)

## Music Resources

- "Cosmetic Fixation," performed by Randy Stonehill, from the CD *Equator*, Myrrh Records, 1983.
- "I'm Accepted," performed by DeGarmo and Key, from the CD *The Pledge*, Benson Records, 1989.
- "Not Perfect," performed by Church of Rhythm, from the CD *Not Perfect*, Pamplin, 1997.
- "Picture Perfect," performed by Michael W. Smith, from the CD *Change Your World*, Reunion, 1993.
- "Unpretty," performed by TLC, from the CD *Fan Mail*, La Face, 1999.

## Materials Needed and Preparation

- ☐ Gather the following items:
  - ❑ Decorations for the gathering space (see the preparation step that follows this materials list)
  - ❑ Masking tape or traffic cones
  - ❑ Assorted articles of clothing and clothing accessories, one for each participant plus extras
  - ❑ Seven copies of resource 18, "'Whata Ya Doin'?' Skit"
  - ❑ Props for the skit on resource 18 (listed on the resource)
  - ❑ Newsprint and markers (optional)
  - ❑ Small mirrors, one for each participant
  - ❑ Wrapping or tissue paper
  - ❑ Reflective music (optional)
  - ❑ A CD player or a tape player (optional)
  - ❑ Refreshments
- ☐ The gathering space needs to be large enough for a relay to take place. Or you might conduct the physical activities outdoors if weather permits.
- ☐ The gathering space should be decorated to reinforce the theme of basing our worth on our appearance. Here are some possibilities:
  - On the walls post fashion catalogs, covers of magazines, pictures of models, and ads that illustrate the cosmetic culture.

- Present an electronic slide show (for example, using PowerPoint) that includes pictures of the items described in the preceding suggestion.
- Display mannequins dressed fashionably.

☐ Before the activity "Fashion Flair Competition," use masking tape or traffic cones to mark a starting line 10–12 feet from the wall on one end of the meeting room.

☐ Assign seven teen leaders the roles in the skit on resource 18. Provide each with a copy of the script in advance and schedule at least one rehearsal.

☐ Recruit a teen leader or a teen participant to give a 5-minute witness talk illustrating the ways God has helped the young person understand her or his worth. To help the recruit prepare, offer the following questions for reflection:
- In what ways have you struggled with your sense of self-worth or your self-image?
- In what ways does the culture influence your self-image?
- How has God helped you see yourself from a different perspective? How has God helped you improve your self-image?
- How has your self-image changed?
- How do you see yourself today?

Review the talk before the meeting. Provide constructive feedback to help ensure an excellent presentation.

☐ Consider noting the questions from the activity "Theme Introduction and Discussion" on newsprint.

☐ You will want to become very familiar with the presentation portion of this session in order to share the message rather than read it.

☐ Gift wrap a small mirror for each participant.

# Procedure

## Team Prayer (15 minutes before start)

Gather the ministry team together in order to get yourselves centered in prayer before the meeting. Begin by reading and reflecting on Romans 8:38–39. As a team pray that all you say and do will reinforce God's incredible love for each young person who walks through the door. Ask God to fill each leader with his love and to help the team communicate that love practically. Pray for the success of each activity and for each person's role in the gathering. Pray that each participant may truly understand his or her incalculable value in God's eyes. Also pray that God's view of each participant will truly change how that individual sees himself or herself, and will become that individual's standard for measuring his or her self-worth and the worth of others. Interpose petitions for Jesus Christ's presence to fill the hearts of those present through each activity and relationship.

## Greeting (10 minutes before start)

Position your ministry team by the entrance doors and throughout the meeting room. Enthusiastically welcome each young person as she or he arrives. Make sure that no participant is standing alone. As you greet the young people, quietly pray that they may leave the gathering filled with the peace of Christ.

## Introduction (5 minutes)

Welcome the group enthusiastically. Your level of excitement will help set the pace and attitude of the participants. Enthusiastic leader = enthusiastic crowd; lethargic leader = lethargic crowd. Help make newcomers especially welcome by making special mention of them. Briefly introduce the theme of the gathering, saying something like this:

- ✦ Hello! My name is *(your name),* and I want to welcome you to *(your program's name).* Thank you for coming this evening. I especially want to welcome any of you who are here for the first time. We are grateful that you joined us.
- ✦ We live in a cosmetic culture that overemphasizes appearance. It's too easy not to measure up to the digitally enhanced photos of models and to feel bad about oneself. The good news is, God has an entirely different reality. This evening's meeting is titled "The Birth of a New Self-Worth."
- ✦ I cannot guarantee that you will walk out of here with an instantaneously transformed self-image, but you will be given the tools needed to build the kind of foundation that a self-image needs in order to withstand the storms of life.

## Opening Prayer (5 minutes)

Offer a simple prayer that both invites God's presence and ties in the theme of the meeting. The following words offer an example:

✦ Lord, we ask you to be present with us this evening. Help us to see ourselves as you see us. Help us to invest in the things that make us truly attractive in your eyes. Guide us in all we do this evening. Amen.

## Connection Mixer (25 minutes)

**1.** Ask the participants each to find a partner. Tell them to choose someone they do not know, or do not know well. Then give the following instructions:

✦ Determine ten things that you and your partner have in common. Find items that are not common to being human—something other than "We both have two feet," for example. You have 5 minutes to complete this task.

**2.** Call for the participants' attention and then offer the next set of instructions:

✦ Join another pair and find ten things that the four of you have in common. You have 5 minutes to complete this task.

**3.** Again call for the participants' attention, and then offer the next set of instructions:

✦ Join another group of four and find eight things that the eight of you have in common. You have 7 minutes to complete this task.

**4.** Finally, combine all the participants into one large group and give them 7 minutes to find three things that they all have in common.

## Fashion Flair Competition (10 minutes)

**1.** Recruit three participants to serve as judges for this activity. Ask them to stand near you. Then divide the remaining participants into teams of six to eight. Tell the teams to designate one member "the mannequin." Have the teams line up behind the starting line at one end of the meeting room, with their mannequins standing directly across from them at the opposite end of the room. In the middle of the room, between each team and its mannequin, place a pile of clothing and clothing accessories.

**2.** Provide the following instructions:

✦ At "Go" one member of each team races to the pile of clothing, selects an item, and runs the item to the team's human mannequin.

✦ The mannequin dresses in the item as quickly as possible.

✦ Once the mannequin is dressed, the team member races back and tags the next team member in line, and that person repeats the steps I just mentioned. The process continues until every team member has given the mannequin a piece of clothing or an accessory.

✦ Once all the mannequins are dressed, they are presented to an unbiased group of judges, who pick the one with the most "fashion flair."

✦ Ultimately each team's tasks are to (1) be the first to finish and (2) pick clothing and accessories that give its mannequin the most fashion flair.

**3.** Conduct the relay as noted in step 2. Once it is concluded, ask the participants to regather as a large group, and announce the winner of the speed portion of the relay. Then invite the mannequins to come forward. Allow the judges a moment to discuss and to determine the first-, second-, and third-place winners. Then ask the judges to announce the top three fashionable mannequins.

## "Whata Ya Doin'?" Skit (10 minutes)

**1.** Offer the following comments in your own words:

✦ Is the saying "Look good. Feel good" true? How much could we feel if feelings were only skin deep? It is easy to get so caught up in looking good that we lose our perspective about what is really important. The following skit illustrates that well.

**2.** Invite the actors you have selected to come forward and present the skit outlined on resource 18. Be sure to thank the actors at the completion of the skit.

## Teen Witness Talk (5 minutes)

**1.** Introduce the teen leader or participant you have invited to share a witness talk.

**2.** At the conclusion of the witness talk, thank the person who has shared and offer any comments you think might help the group move into the next portion of the gathering.

## Theme Introduction and Discussion (10 minutes)

Instruct the participants to gather into teams to discuss two or three of the following questions. You may wish to post these questions on newsprint.

✦ On a scale of 1 to 10 (with 10 being "High" and 1 being "Low"), how do you rate the value our culture places on looks and physical attractiveness? Please explain your rating.

✦ Some people say that most people judge others by the way they look. Do you agree? Why or why not?

✦ Does the "body-image" mentality ("I've got to look good in order to feel good") affect one gender more than the other? Please defend your position.

✦ What do you think most influences a person's view of self?

✦ What do you think is the difference between a person who has a positive self-image and a person who has a negative self-image? How might the two behave differently? What factors lead to a positive self-image? What factors lead to a negative self-image?

✦ Some people say that gatherings of our peers can be like costume balls, where we dress up in false selves in order to be accepted, but feel only more alone because we hide our true selves. Do you agree? Why or why not?

## Keynote Presentation: The Sign of Self-Worth (15 minutes)

Offer the following presentation in your own words:

✦ Sometimes we fail to recognize the value of what we already have. And sometimes that failure affects our lives in a big way. Take, for example, the story of Roy Whetstine, a Texan gemstone broker:

"In 1986, Roy rummaged through numerous containers filled with unpolished stones among the amateur salesmen in an Arizona mineral show. He fished out from a Tupperware dish a dusty, lavender gray rock, about the size of a small potato. After examining it with his well-trained eye, he said to the salesman, 'You want $15 for this rock?' The man replied, 'Tell you what, I'll let you have it for $10. It's not as pretty as the others.' Whetstine forked over $10 and brought home with him what he named the Life and

Pride of America, the largest star sapphire in the world, valued at 2.28 million!" (adapted from Frank Mercadante, *Growing Teen Disciples*, p. 106).

✦ Roy was lucky. But consider the guy who sold him the rock! He gave up his chance to be a multimillionaire for a measly ten bucks. What a tragedy! If only he had recognized what he already possessed! How different his life would be!

✦ That amateur gem salesman's sad reality is similar to many people's experience of life. Many of us fail to recognize our own value. If only we could see our true worth, could see ourselves as God sees us, our lives would be so rich, so different.

✦ The good news is that every person can truly know his or her tremendous worth by taking to heart three realities. Before we examine those realities, we must ask, "What is reality?" Sometimes what we think is true is not. Sometimes what we think is not true is.

✦ During the beginning of the Vietnam War, American pilots traveled to South Vietnam to train the South Vietnamese air force. On one training mission, a young South Vietnamese pilot was flying dangerously close to the ground. His trainer radioed to him to pull the plane up, but he only edged it closer to the ground. Every time his trainer warned him to raise the plane up, he responded by bringing it farther down. On the verge of disaster, the trainer desperately screamed, "Pull it up hard!" The jet suddenly plunged from the sky and burst into a mushroom of flames as it slammed into the rocky terrain. When investigators examined the wreckage, they found that the pilot had struck the ground while streaking upside-down.

✦ The young serviceman had experienced a phenomenon called vertigo. Vertigo can strike when pilots are flying in cloud cover or for some other reason are unable to see the horizon. The result is disorientation. At times they may feel that their aircraft are actually upside-down, and their senses scream to turn the planes "right-side-up." Pilots are trained to always rely on their instrument panels. If the instruments say they are flying right-side-up, then they are right-side-up—no matter what their feelings are telling them.

✦ We, too, need a reliable instrument in order to understand reality—to measure truth, to know who we really are. Like the young pilot, we may get disoriented—we may be distracted by our own feelings or lose perspective in the clouds of our culture. The instrument that God has given us to use for understanding reality and measuring truth is the Scriptures. The truest source of who we are is what the Scriptures say of us. Within the Scriptures we find three realities about who we are that can change our perspective. Those three realities are profoundly simple, but if we take them to heart, their impact on our lives will be simply profound.

✦ The *first reality* is, the Father created you. The Scriptures tell us that we were created by God the Father. Psalm 139 states:

> For it was you who formed my inward parts;
> you knit me together in my mother's womb.
> I praise you for I am fearfully and wonderfully
> made.
>
> (Verses 13–14)

✦ What does that mean? Let's say I place before you two paintings. You can pick one of them to keep. The first painting is the best one I have ever done. My mother is really fond of it. She is really proud of my work, and of me too, of course. The second painting is an original portrait of a woman of the early sixteenth century. She's not all that attractive by today's standards, but the painting is pretty good. I think her name is something like Mona. Mona Lisa. The guy who painted her is dead now. I think his name is Leonardo DiCaprio—no, that's Leonardo da Vinci.

✦ Well, the choice is yours. You can have my painting—if you can peel it from the tenacious grip of my mother's hands. Or you can have this old picture of Mona Lisa. What is your choice?

✦ If you choose my painting, bless your heart, but your fate will differ little from the amateur gem salesman's. Obviously, you should choose the portrait of Mona Lisa, because it was painted by one of the greatest artists this world has ever known, and its worth is directly related to the master who created it.

✦ Now consider who created you—the master creator, the God of the universe. The Father is the master artist, and you are a direct expression of his creativity. Your uniqueness is a result of the eternal master's brushstroke. You are greatly valued, and your worth is immeasurable, because you are a work of the greatest being who ever existed. When the Lord completed creation, he looked it over and said that it was very good (Genesis 1:31)—and it includes you!

✦ You have tremendous worth because the Father created you. To help you take this truth to heart and be constantly reminded of who you are in God's eyes, we are going to tie this concept to a common Catholic gesture. We begin every prayer and every Mass with the sign of the cross—which is made while saying, *(making the gesture)* "In the name of the Father, and of the Son, and of the Holy Spirit." Now, every time you say, "In the name of the Father," remember, the Father created you.

✦ Let's do it together. *(Invite everyone to place their hands on their foreheads and repeat after you.)* "In the name of the Father—the Father created me."

✦ The *second reality* is, the Son died for you. The Scriptures tell us, "For, God so loved the world that he gave his only Son, so that everyone who believes in him may not perish, but may have eternal life" (John 3:16). The Apostle Paul said, "God proves his love for us in that while we were still sinners Christ died for us" (Romans 5:8).

✦ Have you ever lost a Tupperware filled with leftovers in the back of your refrigerator and forgotten all about it? Somehow it ends up hidden for weeks. One day you're starving for lunch and you spot it, hoping for a pleasant gastronomical delight. You pull it out and lift the lid, only to be overcome by a putrid stench of decay that not only takes away your ravenous appetite but also makes you nauseated and queasy. The original contents of the container are unrecognizable under green mold. The only place for this stuff is the garbage. And so you throw it out—not just in the bag under the kitchen sink, but all the way out in the garage, in the big covered garbage can.

To make matters worse, it's hot and humid outside, and it's Tuesday, and the garbage is collected on Mondays. After your leftovers have spent a few days in the garbage, the foul fumes have made the garage uninhabitable. Even the dog, whose water bowl is in there, won't go near it. You try to avoid it too, but one night you have to throw something else in the garbage can.

When you open the lid, you find a colony of filthy maggots swarming in delight upon the lethal substance. Yuck!

Monday rolls around, and you can finally rid yourself of this toxic waste. You hold your breath while carrying the garbage can to the curb. A couple of maggots escape from under the lid and start crawling up your hand. Their bodies are drenched with the moldy, puslike contents of their feast. A wave of nausea overcomes you as you gag and shake your hand violently in an attempt to rid yourself of these filthy pests. Finally, you hear the screech of the garbage truck as it slams its brakes in front of your house. You look at the sanitation engineer as he reaches for your garbage can. . . . And you burst between the garbage man and the garbage, screaming: "Spare the garbage! Let it live! Take me instead! I give my life in behalf of the garbage!"

✦ Is there anyone in this room who would do that? Is there anyone here who would exchange her or his life for garbage? anyone who would die for garbage?

✦ Neither would Jesus Christ. Jesus would not have died for garbage.

✦ As a matter of fact, we are worth Jesus to the Father. God gave his only begotten Son in order to express his unimaginable love for us. The fact that Jesus died for us speaks volumes about our incredible worth in God's eyes. Again, if we take this profoundly simple fact to heart, the impact on our lives will be simply profound.

✦ Again, to help us take this reality to heart, we will tie its truth to the sign of the cross. Let's first review. Repeat after me: *(making the first two gestures in the sign of the cross)* "In the name of the Father—the Father created me. And of the Son—the Son died for me."

✦ The *third reality* is, the Holy Spirit lives within you. The Scriptures say, "Do you not know that you are God's temple, and that God's Spirit dwells in you?" (1 Corinthians 2:16). Through Baptism, the Holy Spirit makes a home in us. God lives and dwells in you and me.

✦ Some of you may be familiar with the MTV show *Cribs* or an older television show, *Lifestyles of the Rich and Famous*. In both series a host walks us through the homes of the very rich and the very famous. The houses are certainly interesting in and of themselves, but what makes them most fascinating and valuable are the people who live in them. As those shows demonstrate, millionaires do not live in worthless shacks, and billionaires do not reside in inexpensive bungalows.

✦ The Holy Spirit, who is an "infinitillionaire," would not dwell in a barren and worthless cave. The Holy Spirit can live only in what God finds valuable and good.

✦ The Holy Spirit lives within you. Because of that, God dwells in you, and you are incredibly valuable. A rich and eternally famous infinitillionaire lives in your heart as a result of your Baptism. And again, if we take this profoundly simple fact to heart, the impact on our lives will be simply profound.

✦ Yet again, to help us take this reality to heart, we will tie its truth to the sign of the cross. Let's first review. Repeat after me: *(making the sign of the cross)* "In the name of the Father—the Father created me. And of the Son—the Son died for me. And of the Holy Spirit—the Holy Spirit lives within me."

✦ There once was a family of prairie chickens that lived on a plain. An egg of an eagle was somehow abandoned near the family's grass nest, and the mother prairie chicken included it as one of her own. After the eagle hatched, she looked a little different from her prairie chicken siblings, but her family accepted her all the same.

Prairie chickens are rather lowly birds. They'll eat garbage, and they can't even fly. Eagles, on the other hand, are the most majestic of birds. They can soar to great heights, flying with a grace and dignity that surpass all others. This eagle, who thought she was a prairie chicken, grew up like a prairie chicken. She walked, squawked, and acted like the rest of her family.

One day an eagle soared above the family of prairie chickens. They picked up their heads and watched in awe the aerial feats of that majestic creature. The eagle who thought she was a prairie chicken turned to her siblings and squawked in astonishment, "Wow, look at that!" Her prairie chicken sisters turned toward her and smugly remarked: "That's an eagle, the greatest of birds. You are just one of us—a lowly prairie chicken."

Sadly, that eagle died believing she was only a prairie chicken. She never thought of lifting her wings and taking flight into the domain for which she had been created. It never occurred to her that she was destined to join the other eagles in the heights of the great blue sky.

✦ You were born an eagle. God has destined you for the heights. He has created you with a dignity befitting only a son or daughter of the eternal Father. You don't have to live and die like the eagle who thought she was a prairie chicken. Taking to heart the truth about who you are can change your life. Believing these three realities can keep you from trying to live out of a false sense of self.

✦ We don't have to play the game of the cosmetic culture—we don't have to buy into the idea that to feel good we have to look good in the eyes of the world around us. We are already created very good and beautiful in the eyes of our Maker. Which opinion is more valuable: the comments of a superficial culture, or the declaration of the Creator of the universe?

✦ The Eternal Maker not only created us by and in his image; he further demonstrated his love by Jesus's death. Jesus was worth everything to the Father; and the Father boldly communicates to us that we are worth everything to him by virtue of Jesus's dying for us.

✦ The Holy Spirit, the third person of the Holy Trinity, resides in us. God has further communicated our worth and value by making his dwelling in our hearts.

✦ Repeat after me: *(making the sign of the cross)* "In the name of the Father—the Father created me. And of the Son—the Son died for me. And of the Holy Spirit—the Holy Spirit lives within me." Whenever you make the sign of the cross, remember who you are in God's eyes.

## Closing Prayer: A Unique Gift (10 minutes)

**1.** Allow a moment of silence to set the tone for closing comments and reflection. Then quietly give each participant a gift-wrapped mirror. Instruct the group not to open their gifts until told. You may wish to play some reflective instrumental music.

**2.** Introduce the closing prayer with these or similar words:

◆ We are concluding this evening by giving each of you a unique, one-of-a-kind gift. Before you open your gifts, I want to read a description of them from their manufacturer:

  ◇ Each gift is unique and distinctive.
  ◇ Each is exclusive, novel, original, and one of a kind. As a matter of fact, after each was made, its mold was broken.
  ◇ Each is indeed special.
  ◇ The worth of each gift cannot be measured in dollars. Each gift is invaluable and precious. Each is indeed priceless.
  ◇ Each of these unique and priceless gifts has a special use. Each was designed with a wonderful plan in mind.
  ◇ Each has a unique intention and purpose, significance and essence. Each is indeed notable.
  ◇ These special, invaluable, and purposeful gifts are brilliant in design.
  ◇ Each is highly technical and complex, from its substance to its essence. Each is indeed sophisticated.
  ◇ These gifts are not mass-produced. The designer remembers and knows each one. Each gift was indeed made in love.

**3.** Instruct the participants to open their unique gifts and look them over carefully.

## Refreshments (15 minutes)

Young people will stick around after the meeting if there is something to eat. Use this postgathering follow-up time to further establish relationships with teens, find out what they thought of the session, and continue to share your faith one-on-one. Remember: the best large-group evangelization does not stand solely on its program but is undergirded by a web of relationships that reinforce the evangelistic message interpersonally.

# "Whata Ya Doin'?" Skit

## Cast

- Four image characters:
  - Clothes Guy (or Girl)
  - Hair Girl (or Guy)
  - Makeup Girl (or Guy)
  - Workout Guy (or Girl)
- Two "whata ya doin'?" characters:
  - Guy
  - Girl
- Normal (a girl or a guy)

## Background

The goal with this skit is to make the "whata ya doin'?" characters look as outrageous and ridiculous as possible. Ham it up! Have fun! It is important to balance the ratio of males to females in the cast. The four image characters should distance themselves from one another physically, to signify separation.

## Props

- *Clothes Guy (or Girl):* Two name-brand shirts or other articles of clothing
- *Hair Girl (or Guy):* Brush, comb, hairdryer, curling iron, hair spray, hair gel, and other hair stuff
- *Makeup Girl (or Guy):* Blush, eye shadow, lipstick, and one clip-on hoop earring
- *Workout Guy (or Girl):* Rolled-up socks for fake muscles, dumbbells, and other types of weights
- *Guy and Girl:* Clothes with pockets, and money in the pockets (fake money is fine)

## Script

*(The scene starts with the four image characters onstage. Guy and Girl enter and approach Clothes Guy.)*

**Girl:** *(to Clothes Guy)* Whata ya doin'?
**Clothes Guy:** *(looking arrogant and in love with self)* I'm wearing Abercrombie. You should try it. *(Clothes Guy holds out two name-brand shirts or other articles of clothing.)*

*(Girl and Guy consult and decide to put on the items he has offered. Clothes Guy immediately rifles through their pockets, taking out any money he finds and leaving the pockets turned inside out.)*

**Girl and Guy:** *(shocked, annoyed, and confused)* Hey! What are you doing?!
**Clothes Guy:** *(matter-of-fact)* These things cost money, man.

*(Girl and Guy leave, confused, and go to Hair Girl.)*

**Guy:** Whata ya doin'?
**Hair Girl:** *(playing with her hair and the hair stuff)* I'm doing my hair. You should try it.

*(Guy and Girl use Hair Girl's tools and products to style their hair. Hair Girl helps. [Remember . . . think outrageous.] The three chatter—adlibbing—during this process.)*

*(Guy and Girl look satisfied with themselves, and Hair Girl is pleased. Guy and Girl move on to Makeup Girl.)*

**Guy:** Whata ya doin'?
**Makeup Girl:** *(applying lipstick and eye shadow)* I'm putting on makeup. You should try it.

*(Girl starts putting on makeup with the help of Makeup Girl. [Again, think outrageous.] Guy watches. He moves around the two of them to view from different angles. He's passively interested. His reactions can provide a good deal of entertainment for the audience.)*

*(When Girl is done, she and Makeup Girl turn to Guy to start making him over.)*

**Guy:**  *(alarmed)* WHAT ARE YOU DOING?!

*(Makeup Girl understands and reaches for the clip-on earring. She puts the earring in Guy's nose like a bull's ring. Girl and Guy look satisfied and move on to Workout Guy.)*

**Girl:**  Whata ya doin'?
**Workout Guy:**  *(lifting the dumbbells and flexing his muscles)* I'm working out. You should try it.

*(Guy and Girl pick up weights and work out. Workout Guy acts as a personal trainer and in the process stuffs the rolled-up socks into their sleeves—the more socks the better. All three look pleased with Guy's and Girl's new "muscles.")*

*(As Guy and Girl leave, Normal walks by.)*

**Girl:**  *(stopping Normal)* Whata ya doin'?
**Normal:**  I'm going to class.

*(Guy and Girl snicker to themselves, as if to say, "The fool doesn't even know what we're talking about!")*

**Guy:**  No, no, no. *(clears throat and pauses)* Whata ya doin'?
**Normal:**  *(a little confused)* I'm going to class.
**Girl:**  *(annoyed, giving a Valley girl sigh and overpronouncing her words)* WHAT ARE YOU DOING?
**Normal:**  *(equally annoyed and also stressing her words)* I'M GOING TO CLASS.

*(Pause.)*

**Normal:**  *(cautiously)* What are *you* doing?

*(Guy and Girl begin talking, each trying to outdo the other, telling her all about the fabulous ways they've improved themselves. They are flamboyant and self-consumed. After a short time, Normal has had enough and walks away while they are still blabbing. As she walks away, Guy and Girl at first keep talking but slowly become quiet so that Normal can deliver her last line.)*

**Normal:**  *(under her breath and to the audience)* I'd rather be going to class.

# Chapter Ten

# Is God a Mirage or the Real Deal?

## Understanding Who God Really Is

### Overview

Many teens misconceive God's character and nature. Often their false ideas can stand as a barrier to knowing God and growing in a relationship with him. Instead of regarding God as an attentive, loving, and caring parent into whose arms they can run, some teens view him as too distant to be concerned about their lives—in other words, as aloof. Others think God delights in finding fault in them and jubilantly meting out the appropriate punishments. Still others see God as a killjoy who issues a divine ban on fun and therefore sentences the believer to holy misery. In this session the participants examine those common misconceptions, and learn more about God's true nature by reflecting on what has been revealed in the Scriptures.

### Objectives

- To identify and understand three common misconceptions of God
- To identify our own misconceptions of God
- To understand God's true character and nature as revealed in the Scriptures
- To prayerfully respond to God's love and his call to a deeper relationship with Jesus Christ

### Themes
- Common misconceptions of God
- God's true character and nature

### Schedule
- Pregathering Hospitality
  - Team Prayer (15 minutes before start)
  - Greeting (10 minutes before start)
- Welcome
  - Introduction and Opening Prayer (5 minutes)
  - First-Impressions Mixer (15 minutes)
- Warm-Up
  - Cheese-Ball Toss (15 minutes)
- Message
  - "Who Is God?" Discussion (15 minutes)
  - "Is God a Mirage or the Real Deal?" Skit (5 minutes)
  - Theme Introduction and Discussion (10 minutes)
  - Keynote Presentation: Is God a Mirage or the Real Deal? (15 minutes)
- Closure
  - Closing Prayer: Open-the-Door Invitation (5 minutes)
- Postgathering Follow-Up
  - Refreshments (15 minutes)

## Scripture Passage

Bless the Lord, O my soul and all that is within me,
bless his holy name!
Bless the Lord, O, my soul; do not forget all his benefits—,
Who forgives all your iniquity, who heals all your
   diseases?
Who redeems your life from the Pit,
Who crowns you with steadfast love and mercy,
Who satisfies you with good as long as you live
So that your youth is renewed like the eagle's.

(Psalm 103:1–5)

## Music Resources

- "God Is Love," performed by John Reuben, from the CD *Are We There Yet?* Gotee Records, 2000.
- "Jesus Is God," performed by Scarecrow and Tinmen, from the CD *Superhero*, Organic Records, 2000.
- "Ocean," performed by Ten Shekel Shirt, from the CD *Much*, Verticle Music, 2001.
- "Universe," performed by Rebecca St. James, from the CD *Transform*, ForeFront/Emd Records, 2000.
- "Who Is This?" performed by The Insyderz, from the CD *Skalleluia Too!* KMG Records, 1999.

## Materials Needed and Preparation

☐ Gather the following items:
  ☐ Decorations for the gathering space (see the preparation step that follows this materials list)
  ☐ Copies of handout 2, "First-Impressions Mixer," one for each participant
  ☐ Pencils or pens, one for each participant
  ☐ Masking tape
  ☐ Chairs, one for each team of ten
  ☐ Cheese balls, eight for each participant
  ☐ Large trash bags with a head-sized hole cut in the bottom center, one for each team of ten
  ☐ Shower caps, one for each team of ten
  ☐ Goggles, one for each team of ten
  ☐ One can of nonmenthol shaving cream
  ☐ A watch, clock, or timer
  ☐ Ten sheets of blank paper
  ☐ Markers

- ❏ Six copies of resource 19, "'Is God a Mirage or the Real Deal?' Skit"
- ❏ Props for the skit on resource 19 (listed on the resource)
- ❏ Newsprint (optional)
- ❏ Reflective music
- ❏ A CD player or a tape player
- ❏ A flashlight or a spotlight
- ❏ A door that has a knob on only one side

☐ The meeting room should be decorated to reinforce the theme of God's true character and attributes. One possibility is to display Scripture quotes that depict God's character, especially those used in the activity "Keynote Presentation: Is God a Mirage or the Real Deal?"

☐ Use masking tape to create two lines across the floor about 8–10 feet apart. Along one line, evenly spaced, place chairs facing the other line, one chair for each team of ten in the "Cheese-Ball Toss" activity.

☐ On separate sheets of paper, write in large print the numbers 1 to 10.

☐ Choose six participants or teen leaders to present the skit from resource 19. Provide them each with a copy of the resource so that they can prepare in advance.

☐ Consider noting the questions from the activity "Theme Introduction and Discussion" on newsprint.

☐ You will want to become very familiar with the presentation portion of this session in order to share the message rather than read it.

☐ Stand the door with one knob securely in the stage area of the meeting room, positioned so that the audience can see both sides.

# Procedure

## Team Prayer (15 minutes before start)

Gather the ministry team together in order to get yourselves centered in prayer before the meeting. Begin by reading and reflecting on 1 Thessalonians 1:5. Then invite the team to pray that the Lord will powerfully touch the heart of each teen attending. Pray for the success of each activity and for each person's role in the gathering.

## Greeting (10 minutes before start)

Position your ministry team by the entrance doors and throughout the meeting room. Enthusiastically welcome each young person as she or he arrives. Make sure that no participant is standing alone. As you greet the young people, pray for them quietly.

## Introduction and Opening Prayer (5 minutes)

**1.** Welcome the group enthusiastically. Your level of excitement will help set the pace and attitude of the participants. Help make newcomers especially welcome by making special mention of them. Briefly introduce the theme of the gathering, saying something like this:

✦ Welcome! My name is *(your name)*, and I want to welcome you to *(your program's name)*. I am grateful that you are with us this evening. I especially want to welcome any of you who are here for the first time. We are honored that you have joined us.

✦ This evening's theme is "Is God a Mirage or the Real Deal?" We're going to look at some of the popular but inaccurate ways we view God, and compare them with who God is according to the Scriptures.

**2.** Invite the participants to join you in saying the sign of the cross. Then offer a simple prayer that invites God's presence and ties in the theme of the meeting, such as this example:

✦ Lord, we invite you to be with us here. Please help us to know you as you really are. Help us to let go of misconceptions we have of you that may keep us from a close relationship with you. We ask this in Jesus's name. Amen.

## First-Impressions Mixer (15 minutes)

**1.** Distribute handout 2, and pencils or pens. Ask the participants to find a person with whom they are not yet well acquainted, to exchange names with that person if necessary, and to sit quietly with him or her. Then tell the young people to complete the handout individually, using their first impressions of their partners. Allow about 5 minutes for them to complete the task.

**2.** Invite the partners to share their first impressions with each other and to follow up by exchanging the real answer to each question. Direct them to finish by comparing their answers to see how accurate they were.

**3.** Conclude by asking for a show of hands as to how many questions were answered correctly. Then offer these or similar comments:

✦ Our impressions of others are not always correct, as this game illustrates well. Only after learning about another person can we know who he or she is.

✦ The same is true with God. Often we have impressions or conceptions of God that do not reflect God's true character. It is only after learning who God really is that we can really know the Lord.

## Cheese-Ball Toss (15 minutes)

**1.** Divide the participants into teams of ten. Ask the teams to line up behind the masking tape line that does not have chairs along it, facing the line of chairs, with each team directly across from one of the chairs. Tell the participants this:

✦ We are going to play a game called "Cheese-Ball Toss." The simple object of the game is for your team's designated cheese-ball catcher to catch the most cheese balls.

✦ Each team needs to choose one person to serve as its catcher. That person should not be allergic to nonmenthol shaving cream. *(Allow a minute for the teams to make this determination.)*

✦ Each catcher should now be seated in the chair on the line across from your team.

✦ The rest of you are to line up single file behind the tape line, facing your seated catcher.

**2.** Give each participant eight cheese balls. Then inform the catchers that there is one final detail. Provide each with a precut trash bag. Tell the catchers that instead of grabbing the cheese balls with their hands, they have to grab them with their faces. Explain that the catchers should place their garbage bags over their heads so that their bodies are covered but their heads come through the opening. Provide them with shower caps to place over their heads. Also provide them with goggles to place over their eyes. Finally, explain that you will thickly lather their faces and foreheads with shaving cream. (Check with each catcher to make sure she or he is still willing to be a catcher, and to be certain none of the catchers have any allergies or skin conditions that might be irritated by the shaving cream.)

**3.** Tell the remaining team members to take turns tossing their cheese balls to their catchers. The goal is for a cheese ball to attach itself to the catcher's shaving cream–packed face. Tell the participants that a point will be awarded for each cheese ball that stays on their catcher's face. The team with the most attached cheese balls when you call time wins.

Ask the participants if any of the instructions you have just given need to be clarified or repeated. Respond accordingly. Conduct the game as noted, call time after about 5 minutes, and then help the participants clean up.

## "Who Is God?" Discussion (15 minutes)

**1.** Place ten numbered sheets of paper in consecutive order on the floor in the front of the room, leaving 2-foot spaces between the sheets. Then call for six to eight volunteers to respond to a series of statements. Explain that you will ask the volunteers to stand by the number that best corresponds to the intensity of their agreement or disagreement with each statement: the number 1 indicates "I totally disagree"; the number 10 means "I totally agree."

**2.** Ask the audience to observe the volunteers' responses to each statement. Then read the first of the round 1 statements. Allow time for the volunteers to complete their movements. Give the audience a minute to ask questions regarding the volunteers' choices. Continue in the same manner with the remaining round 1 statements.

After round 1 is completed, begin round 2 by inviting a new group of volunteers to come forward. The statements for both rounds are listed below.

### Round 1 Statements
- God is all-loving.
- God is perfectly just in his judgment.
- God created hell, and some people will spend eternity there.
- God is all-forgiving and all-merciful.
- God will hold us accountable for our actions.
- All people will go to heaven.
- I have fully committed my life to God.

**Round 2 Statements**

- God is not interested in all the details of our lives.
- God loves us and has our best interests in mind.
- Committing our lives to Jesus Christ is one of life's greatest adventures.
- Anyone can have an intimate relationship with God.
- Being a good Christian is boring.
- God answers all our prayers.
- I have committed my life to Christ, and I am experiencing a very close relationship with God.

## "Is God a Mirage or the Real Deal?" Skit (5 minutes)

**1.** Introduce this portion of the gathering with these or similar words:

- ✦ At the beginning of our gathering, when we played "First-Impressions Mixer," you may have experienced some misconceptions of your partner.
- ✦ When our catchers in "Cheese-Ball Toss" volunteered, they were probably under the impression that they would be catching cheese balls with their hands and not with their lathered faces.
- ✦ Life is full of misconceptions—wrong impressions of someone or something. The following skit depicts some common misconceptions of God.

**2.** Invite the actors you have selected to come forward and present the skit from resource 19. Be sure to thank them at the completion of the skit.

## Theme Introduction and Discussion (10 minutes)

Instruct the participants to gather into teams of ten to discuss two or three of the following questions. You may wish to post these questions on newsprint.

- ✦ What are the most common perceptions or misperceptions of God? Why, do you think, do people perceive God in those ways?
- ✦ Where do you get your knowledge of who God is?
- ✦ Where can you get accurate or reliable information about the nature of God?
- ✦ Of the three misconceptions represented in the skit, which relates best to your experience?
- ✦ Who is God in your life?
- ✦ What role does God play in your life?

## Keynote Presentation:
## Is God a Mirage or the Real Deal? (15 minutes)

Offer the following presentation in your own words:

✦ A man was once visiting New York City. The staff at his hotel told him to be very careful in Central Park because recently there had been several muggings. An avid jogger, he went out for some exercise, and he sort of by accident ended up in Central Park. The sun had just set, and it was just getting dark. The warnings of the hotel staff echoed in his mind as he saw a man jogging toward him. The man bumped into him, and continued on his way without a word of apology. The man from out of town chalked it up to big-city rudeness. A few seconds later, he reached for his wallet and realized that it was missing! He resolutely refused to be a victimized tourist, so he turned around and sprinted after the man who had bumped him. Uncharacteristically, this normally easy-going visitor caught the mugger, threw him to the ground, retrieved the wallet, and sprinted back to the hotel.

Reaching the safety of his hotel, the out-of-towner couldn't believe that he had actually been pickpocketed. He felt unnerved by the violation. He felt no guilt whatsoever about having taken the criminal down and retrieved what was his.

The man returned to his room and sat down on his bed to take off his jogging shoes. His eyes lit on the pants he had worn earlier that day. To his surprise, there was a bulge in the back pocket. Grabbing the pants, he searched the pocket, and sure enough, there was his wallet! As the realization of his mistake dawned on him, he got a sick feeling in the pit of his stomach. Instead of being mugged, he had actually been the mugger! He was jarred from his nausea by a pounding at his door: "Open up; New York City police."

✦ Misunderstandings can be costly! A man was driving a friend who had recently had his appendix removed. As the driver approached an intersection, he asked his friend, "How's your side?" The friend replied, "It's fine." The driver pulled into the intersection, and his vehicle was struck on the passenger side by a skidding car. Exasperated, the driver yelled, "I thought you said your side was good!" The shaken passenger answered:

"I thought you meant my side where I had my surgery. It's healing well."

✦ As costly as those two misconceptions were, they pale in comparison with the cost of misunderstanding God's character. Mistaking God's character in a way that prevents us from knowing the Lord personally and intimately is the most tragic misconception possible. The individual who misreads God's character and dismisses the possibility of a radically different life is like the person who misreads the numbers on a $100 million lottery ticket and discards it. Sadly, people dismiss God all too frequently. Misconceptions of God abound and ultimately have the power to rob us of life as it was meant to be.

✦ Misunderstanding God's character and intentions is nothing new. The first misconception of God was introduced with the first lie uttered on the earth. In Genesis 3:1–5, the serpent lies to Adam and Eve. He tries to get them to doubt God's good intentions for them.

✦ The evil one wants us to believe that God does not have our best interests in mind and is holding back the best from us. The serpent of old despises God and knows that the best way of getting back at the Lord is by hurting those whom the Lord passionately loves. The most effective way of hurting a mother or a father is not by attacking her or him but by harming her or his child.

✦ We were created for intimacy with God. The Lord's plan for each of us is to be close to him. That ache we feel, that emptiness, that "missing something" is our soul's search for its Maker. The best way to keep a soul from the Lord is to paint God's character with colors of deception. The three common misconceptions represented in the earlier skit depict a God that doesn't exist. Let's take a closer look at the mirages of God and come to a better understanding of the real deal.

✦ The *first mirage* presents God as aloof, or distant. This God is generally inaccessible. This God lost interest in our affairs after winding the clock of our universe. That becomes painfully apparent on our sixteenth birthday when we fail to find that brand-new Ferrari in the driveway after fervently praying for it the night before.

Somehow, we realize, our desperate plea got lost en route to a God who resides about a billion light-years away. No new Ferrari—no caring God. God is uninterested in our lives, we despondently conclude.

◆ The Bible speaks of a very different God. The Lord of the Scriptures is fully aware of even the most minute details of our lives. In Luke 12:7, Jesus tells us not to be afraid because even all the hairs on our heads are counted by God.

◆ Jesus is saying that God is so intimately aware of our lives that he notices something as insignificant as a fallen hair. Well, maybe that isn't so insignificant if you're going bald in your twenties—but you get the picture! God cares deeply about us! In actuality, details of our lives that may escape our notice don't escape God's. In reality, God cares more for us than we care for ourselves!

◆ Sometimes, when our lives are difficult, we can think that God somehow forgot us with everything else going on. Every one of us has been let down to some degree by others. People have forgotten us—even people who care about us.

◆ Once a father of four dropped off his wife and their three small children at the door of the church for Mass. He told his wife that he would park the car and join them with their youngest, an infant in a car seat.

Proud of himself for finding a relatively close parking space, the man locked the car and hurried to join his family. As he searched the congregation, he finally caught a glimpse of his wife. Her anxious expression concerned him; he wondered what could have happened in the moments that they had been separated. Her expression went from anxiety to anger to almost terror; he quickened his pace. When he arrived at the pew she frantically looked at him and said, "Where's the baby!?"

◆ Fortunately, God does not become distracted when it comes to his children. Isaiah 49:14–16 says: "Zion said, 'The Lord has forsaken me, my Lord has forgotten me.' Can a woman forget her nursing child, or show no compassion for the child of her womb? Even these may forget, yet I will not forget you. See, I have inscribed you on the palms of my hands." God cannot forget us.

✦ Even when we have no interest in God, or have turned our backs on him, he still looks for us with the longing of a father or mother estranged from a child. The Scriptures illustrate that truth in the parable of the prodigal son. The son knowingly rejects his father and the good life that the father has given him. After taking off and spending all his money and hitting rock bottom, he comes to his senses and heads back home. He figures he is no longer worthy of being considered a son, but being a slave in his father's house would be better than what he has been experiencing.

    While the son is still a long way from home, his father catches sight of him and is filled with compassion (Luke 15:20). Why does the father catch sight of his son while he is so far away? Because the father has spent his waking moments scouring the horizon, hoping to see a glimpse of the young man heading back to his love. And when the father sees his son, he is so overjoyed that he loses every semblance of paternal dignity. He bursts into a mad sprint toward the object of his love.

✦ Those familiar with Middle Eastern culture know that the father was acting crazy! It would have been extremely rare for a father to run toward his son, especially a son who had ungratefully left home. Jesus is trying to teach us that when we stray, God attentively anticipates our return, and when we turn toward God, we will be met with unconditional love and generosity (Luke 15:11–32).

✦ In the reality of life, sometimes we wonder if God really cares. It is true that not all our prayers are answered. And thank God for that! God loves us enough to give us not what we think we need but what he knows we need. Sometimes we may not understand, but we can be assured of God's goodness.

✦ It is also true that God knows our needs before we even ask. We might rightly wonder, "Then why doesn't God just take care of things rather than our having to pray about everything?" If God operated that way, we would have no need for him. Voicing our needs draws us into a relationship with God just as hunger draws us into a search for food. Often, difficult situations are vehicles for developing a relationship with God. And once we come to God, we find that he invites us to throw our burdens on him so that he can show us how much he cares for us. First Peter 5:7 says, "Cast all your anxiety on him, because he cares for you." A friend might listen to our burdens, but God actually relieves us of them. God exchanges our burdens for rest: "Come to me, all you that are weary and are carrying heavy burdens, and I will give you rest. Take my yoke upon you, and learn from me; for I am gentle and humble in heart, and you will find rest for your souls" (Matthew 11:28–29).

✦ Is our God distant and aloof? Absolutely not! God wants to be involved in every detail of our lives and invites us to know him intimately.

✦ The *second mirage* portrays God as a sinister judge who delights in punishing us. This God towers over us, waiting for us to mess up so that he can strike us with lightning and punish us forever with his wrath. This God is a loveless, impossible-to-please, cosmic disciplinarian. Is this the God of the Scriptures?

✦ Let's allow the Scriptures to speak for themselves.

✦ The Lord doesn't want anyone to be punished but wants all to come to the truth. "For God has destined us not for wrath, but for obtaining salvation through our Lord Jesus Christ, who died for us, so that whether we are awake or asleep we may live with him" (1 Thessalonians 5:9–11).

✦ God rejoices in our turning to him and finding life. "Have I any pleasure in the death of the wicked, says the Lord GOD, and not rather that they should turn from their ways and live?" (Ezekiel 18:23). "For I have no pleasure in the death of anyone, says the Lord GOD. Turn, then, and live" (verse 32).

✦ No one is randomly sent to hell. No one ends up separated from God without great effort. If people end up in the bottomless pit, they climbed there themselves, hurdling every protective barrier that God placed in their paths. Throughout our lives God presents numerous opportunities for us to respond to his love. Sometimes he uses gentle invitations, such as a moving homily, the words of our parents, or a quiet but powerful spiritual hunger for God. Other times he issues jarring wake-up calls, such as a warning from a friend or a difficult circumstance. And sometimes he shouts out deafening alarms, like a tragic death of a peer.

✦ We all have opportunities to open the doors of our hearts to Jesus Christ, who wants to bring us life now and forever, but he will not push his way into our lives. "Listen!" he says. "I am standing at the door, knocking; if you hear my voice and open the door, I will come in to you and eat with you, and you with me" (Revelation 3:20). If we choose life apart from God, or hell, we have hurdled every barrier and ignored every opportunity that God has put in our way.

✦ The *third mirage* features God as a cosmic killjoy. This mirage is probably the most popular one these days. The motto goes, "Know God, no fun." People tend to think: If I give my life to God, he'll ruin it. I'll be miserable. I may avoid going to hell, but this life will almost seem like hell. Being a good Catholic is at best boring.

✦ No wonder we have that impression. We may go to Mass on Sunday and look around at the faces in the sanctuary and think, Everyone looks miserable! People don't appear to be enthusiastic and excited about their faith. Besides, it seems like sinners have more fun. All the Church's rules and regulations are outdated and only sentence us to "holy misery."

✦ Sometimes we can be under the illusion that God's rules are restrictive and their only purpose is to prevent us from having a good time. However, for every negative commandment (in other words, for every time God says "No"), there are always two positive purposes. The first is to protect us. God wants to shelter us from the pain and consequences of activities that will hurt us.

✦ A toddler might try to put a paper clip into an electrical socket. A negligent mother might say, "Come on, everyone; let's watch Jenna get shocked and see how loud she cries!" We know that a good mother will do everything in her power to keep her child away from the danger of an electrical socket. In the same way, God uses commandments like "Do not commit adultery" and "Do not steal" to protect us.

✦ The boundaries that God sets for us are meant not to constrain us but to protect us. The boundaries of a river help it flow freely without being a detriment to others. When the boundaries are removed, a flood results and often brings devastation instead of life. God has given us the Scriptures and Church teaching to set some boundaries. When we ignore them, we often hurt others and are unhappy ourselves. For example, Jesus says: "Take care! Be on your guard against all kinds of greed; for one's life does not consist in the abundance of possessions" (Luke 12:15). If we disregard that warning and spend our lives amassing things to make us happy, we'll eventually find that those things leave us empty. Rather, life is found in relationships—with God, with family, with friends.

✦ God issues negative commandments not only to protect us from unnecessary pain but for a second positive purpose: to provide for us. God wants us to experience the best possible lives. God has a great adventure for us now. Walking with Jesus Christ is the most exciting existence this earth has to offer. Eternity begins not with our deaths but when Jesus Christ becomes the center of our lives. We don't have to wait until we die to enjoy closeness with God and blessings that he wants to give to us.

✦ God created us and knows best how we will be happy. The Holy Spirit inspired the "owner's manual" for Christian faith, the Scriptures, to teach us how God meant for us to live. The Lord knows how we work. When God says "No," he always does so with the intention to make us happy, not unhappy. God loves us more than any person ever can, and he truly wants us to be free and happy in Christ.

✦ We have a God who is closer than we can imagine and is calling us, even now. He is the "real deal" and doesn't want us chasing after empty mirages that leave us thirsty for real life. He stands at the doors of our hearts and knocks. He wants to come into our lives and show us his love, to give us the joy that comes from being close to him and the peace that only he can bring. Jesus Christ calls us to a great adventure in following him in this life and being with him forever in the next.

Move right into the closing prayer, as though the talk is actually continuing.

## Closing Prayer: Open-the-Door Invitation (5 minutes)

**1.** Begin by playing some soft, reflective instrumental music in the background. Dim the lights. Shine a flashlight or a spotlight on the door with a knob on only one side, and position yourself near the door.

**2.** Share the following words or something similar:

✦ I invite you to respond to Jesus Christ's knocking.

✦ *(Stand by the door and point out the knob.)* There is only one doorknob, and it is on your side.

✦ Jesus Christ is on the outside of the door, knocking. *(Knock on the side without the doorknob.)*

✦ Jesus Christ is knocking on the doors of our hearts.

✦ *(Move to the side of the door with the knob.)* Sometimes we stand on this side of the door, wavering, thinking: "Jesus Christ, I'm afraid to let you in because I don't want to be miserable. I'm afraid that if I follow you, I won't have any fun. I'm afraid that I won't be able to do the things I want to do."

✦ But those fears are only illusions that keep us from experiencing the incredible love of our God and the abundant life he destined for us. Jesus Christ invites you to open the door of your heart and let him gently show you his goodness.

✦ Take the next few minutes to silently speak to Jesus Christ. Tell him your fears, your worries, your hopes, and your desires. Allow him to speak to your heart.

**3.** Continue with several minutes of personal reflection. End with a spontaneous prayer thanking God for his love and asking for his guidance in making him the center of life.

## Refreshments (15 minutes)

Young people will stick around after the meeting if there is something to eat. Use this postgathering follow-up time to further establish relationships with teens, find out what they thought of the session, and continue to share your faith one-on-one. Remember: the best large-group evangelization does not stand solely on its program but is undergirded by a web of relationships that reinforce the evangelistic message interpersonally.

# First-Impressions Mixer

Find someone you have never met or hardly know. Exchange names, but say no more. Your leader will ask you to quietly answer the following questions using only your first impressions of your partner. When your leader directs you to, share your predictions with your partner and determine how close you were to the truth.

What is your partner's personality?

_____

_____

_____

What is your partner's role in her or his family (birth order, function, method for getting along with siblings and parents, and so forth)?

_____

_____

_____

What is your partner's favorite style of music? Who is her or his favorite musician?

_____

_____

_____

What does your partner hope to be doing ten years from now? (Describe her or his profession or career, marital status, children, living location, and so forth.)

_____

_____

_____

What motivates your partner to be attending this gathering?

_____

_____

_____

  **Handout 2:** Permission to reproduce is granted. © 2004 by Cultivation Ministries.

# "Is God a Mirage or the Real Deal?" Skit

## Cast

- Narrator
- God
- Hurt
- Tempted
- Lighting technician
- Fun-Lover

## Props

- A throne
- A large nail file
- A headset

## Script

**Narrator:** The following drama illustrates three of the most common misconceptions young people have of God. Can you see yourself in any of our characters?

*(God is sitting on his throne. He projects a majestic image that radiates arrogance and aloofness. Hurt walks in with a desperate look and stride, and kneels before God.)*

*(During the following monologue, God looks bored and disinterested. He files his nails at first. He begins to yawn and then dozes and finally enters a deep sleep accompanied by a snore.)*

**Hurt:** Dear God. I really need some help. Things really suck. Mom's pregnant again and that makes ten of us kids now and Dad just lost his job. There's no food in the house and no money coming in. To top it off, kids keep picking on me in school. . . . Man, that hurts. . . . God, are you listening to me? Do you care about me? Are you sleeping up there?! *(Hurt buries head in hands and desperately slumps to the floor and freezes.)*

*(After a few seconds, Tempted walks in. This teen is guilt-laden and ashamed and has a hard time lifting her or his head. Tempted kneels before God. God has a sinister expression and seems to enjoy the agony Tempted is in.)*

**Tempted:** God, I, I really blew it again. I wanted to be strong, but with all my friends drinking, I fell into it again. I got drunk, God. I am really sorry—
**God:** *(interrupting angrily)* WHAT!?

*(The lighting technician turns the room or stage lights on and off like lightning.)*

*(Tempted freezes in position.)*

*(A few seconds pass, and Fun-Lover arrives before God. Fun-Lover has a headset on and is dancing to the music during the approach. God is clearly not amused by this young person's enjoyment.)*

**God:** Hey, you!

*(Fun-Lover cannot hear God because of the headset. God stands up with a poker face.)*

**God:** Hey. Kid. . . . I am talking to you.
**Fun-Lover:** Uh. You talking to me?
**God:** Yeah. Are you having fun?
**Fun-Lover:** Yeah! *(excitedly)* I got this new—
**God:** *(interrupting)* Do you love me?
**Fun-Lover:** Well, of course, Lord.
**God:** Then you cannot have fun.
**Fun-Lover:** But, Lord—
**God:** Fun is the creation of the devil. Is he your model for living?
**Fun-Lover:** Um. No, Lord, uh—
**God:** Good. But if you forget, then let that person stand as a reminder of the devil's ways *(points to the kneeling Tempted)*. Now get rid of that music and get down on your knees and begin the labor of prayer.

**Resource 19:** Permission to reproduce is granted. © 2004 by Cultivation Ministries.

**Fun-Lover:** *(glances fearfully at Tempted and falls to his or her knees and takes off the headset)* Yes, Lord.

*(Fun-Lover and God freeze.)*

**Narrator:** Those were three common misconceptions that many young people have of God.

**Narrator:** *(walks to Hurt)* This scene portrayed an aloof God: a God who doesn't listen to you when you pray and quite frankly doesn't care.

**Narrator:** *(walks to Tempted)* This was a gotcha God: a God who is just waiting for you to make one mistake so that he can experience the pleasure of sending you to hell.

**Narrator:** *(walks to Fun-Lover)* This was a killjoy God: a God who won't let you have any fun and who sentences the believer to a life of boredom and holy misery.

**Narrator:** *(to audience)* Now we're going to show you a more scripturally accurate perspective of who God is.

*(During the following prayer, God comes down from his throne and looks compassionately at Hurt.)*

**Hurt:** *(unfreezes)* Dear God. I really need some help. Things really suck. Mom's pregnant again and that makes ten of us kids now and Dad just lost his job. There's no food in the house and no money coming in. To top it off, kids keep picking on me in school. . . . Man, that hurts—

**God:** Hurt, I know you're going through a rough time, and I want you to know that I will be here for you and your family. You can rely on me to get you through the hard times. When you ask for a loaf of bread, I will never give you a stone.

*(Hurt looks relieved and encouraged, and freezes with a joyful expression.)*

**Tempted:** *(unfreezes)* God, I, I really blew it again. I wanted to be strong, but with all my friends drinking, I fell into it again. I got drunk, God. I am really sorry—

**God:** Tempted, I forgive you. When you are struggling, rely on my strength to pull you through. Be confident that I stand ready to clothe you with strength in the face of temptation. Welcome home, my child.

*(Fun-Lover unfreezes, listens to the music in the headset, then sees God and stops suddenly.)*

**God:** What's the matter?

**Fun-Lover:** Well, isn't it a sin to have fun when you're a Christian?!

**God:** Of course not! I am the creator of fun, but the evil one has taken my creation and perverted it. He has influenced many with the notion that to have fun you must sin. It is your birthright as my child to have fun and enjoy the life I give to you to the fullest. Hey, do you like parties? Heaven is a big party, and everyone's invited.

# Acknowledgments

The scriptural quotations contained herein are taken from the New Revised Standard Version of the Bible, Catholic Edition. Copyright © 1993 and 1989 by the Division of Christian Education of the National Council of Churches of Christ in the United States of America. All rights reserved. Used with permission.

The quote "It's a sin to bore a kid with the Bible," on page 10, is from Young Life, at *www.younglife.org,* accessed July 22, 2004. Copyright © 2003.

Much of chapter 1, the section "Using Team Competition," on pages 42–45, and the story about Roy Whetstine on pages 155–156 are adapted from *Growing Teen Disciples: Strategies for Really Effective Youth Ministry,* by Frank Mercadante (Winona, MN: Saint Mary's Press, 2002), chapter 8, pages 170–172, and page 106, respectively. Copyright © 1998 by Cultivation Ministries. All rights reserved.

The quote "essential mission of the church," on page 45, is from the apostolic exhortation *On Evangelization in the Modern World (Evangelii Nuntiandi),* by Pope Paul VI, section 14, page 8, at *www.vatican.va/holy _father/paul_vi/apost_exhortations/documents/hf_p-vi_exh_19751208 _evangelii-nuntiandi_en.html,* accessed August 2, 2004.

The quote "new evangelization" and extract on page 45 are from *Novo Millennio Ineunte of His Holiness Pope John Paul II to the Bishops, Clergy, and Lay Faithful at the Close of the Great Jubilee of the Year 2000* (Boston: Pauline Books and Media, 2001), section 40, page 52. Copyright © 2001 by the Daughters of Saint Paul.

Resources 5, 6, 7, and 9 are adapted from *Training for Strategic Youth Ministry Training Workbook,* by Cultivation Ministries (Saint Charles, IL: Cultivation Ministries, 1991), pages 15, 13, 46, and 47, respectively. Copyright © 1991–2003 by Cultivation Ministries. All rights reserved. Used with permission.

Resource 10 is adapted from *Cultivation Strategy Workbook: Tools for Really Effective Parish Youth Ministry,* by Cultivation Ministries (Saint Charles, IL: Cultivation Ministries, 2001), pages 6.10–6.14. Copyright © 2001 by Cultivation Ministries. Used with permission.

The story about the chicken on page 90 is adapted from one by Buddy Hackett as retold in "A Three-Legged Chicken!" on Brad Templeton's Rec.Humor.Funny Web site, at *www.netfunny.com/rhf/jokes/91q4/hrdchick.html,* accessed August 2, 2004.

Resource 11 is based on "The Three Little Pigs," in *English Fairy Tales,* by Joseph Jacobs (New York: Alfred A. Knopf, 1890), pages 73–76.

To view copyright terms and conditions for Internet materials cited here, log on to the home pages for the referenced Web sites.

During this book's preparation, all citations, facts, figures, names, addresses, telephone numbers, Internet URLs, and other pieces of information cited within were verified for accuracy. The authors and Saint Mary's Press staff have made every attempt to reference current and valid sources, but we cannot guarantee the content of any source, and we are not responsible for any changes that may have occurred since our verification. If you find an error in, or have a question or concern about, any of the information or sources listed within, please contact Saint Mary's Press.

## Endnote Cited in
### On Evangelization in the Modern World

1. *"Declaration of the Synod Fathers,"* 4: L'Osservatore Romano (27 October 1974), p. 6.

# Endorsements

In *Make It Real,* Frank Mercadante provides a practical, step-by-step process for effective large-group evangelization. From hospitality through the actual gathering to postgathering follow-up, this resource details the planning, implementation, and evaluation needed for creative events, including a description of the various leadership roles. And the six sample sessions already developed are a bonus. *Make It Real* will be valuable for ministry coordinators either as a primary youth ministry approach or as a supplement to an ongoing catechetical / youth ministry program.

Robert J. McCarty
Executive Director
National Federation for Catholic Youth Ministry

*Make It Real: A Practical Resource for Teen-Friendly Evangelization* is not just a book with great ideas. The voice of author Frank Mercadante's years of experience comes through loud and clear, challenging our present methods of ministry. The knowledge gained through these pages can save you time and frustration. You can trust that every practical suggestion has already been through the trial-and-error stage. Readers are challenged to set a high standard when it comes to evangelizing teens, and the content will help them to do just that. This book is like an oyster containing a beautiful pearl. Open it to see!

Lisa Walker and Steve Walker
Cofounders/Copresidents
Catholic Heart Workcamp

During parish visits, I hear again and again the need to be more responsive to young people in their relationship with the Church. This text will be of immeasurable value to those involved with young people. It is practical, usable, and grounded in a faith perspective. The text provides a concrete approach for inviting young people into an active involvement with the Church.

Most Rev. Gerald F. Kicanas, DD
Bishop of Tucson, Arizona